Inside
Indy Car Racing
1991

By Rick Amabile

Library of Congress catalog card number: 90-80544

ISBN # 0-9622382-2-8

Printed in the United States of America

Additional copies can be ordered from:

P.O. Box 25156 • Fresno, CA 93729

Cover Photo of Al Unser, Jr. by Dan Boyd

Luyendyk-Rahal Photo by Ray Aultenschulte - IMS

INTRODUCTION

What you are about to read is a very refreshing book. Like my previous works, this book is designed to provide inside information that was never available to the general public, until I got involved.

This second edition of *Inside Indy Car Racing* represents a change in direction from my previous books. To make the book more personable, I set out to interview various people that comprise the Indy car fraternity. These are the people who I thought might be particularly interesting to talk with.

"What It Costs To Do Indy" is without a doubt the most detailed presentation ever written. This section required a tremendous amount of information gathering, but that's why I write these books, to deliver a never seen before perspective.

Although some drivers are often interviewed in various periodicals, I thought that I would come up with some interesting questions in my own style to create the "One-On-One" interview section of the book.

My favorite section is " Tales From The Road ". I hope that you laugh as hard at some of the stories as I did.

On the other hand, safety has always been the most serious aspect of motor racing. I went behind the scenes to get a different perspective with various safety personnel.

" Inside Lola Cars 1991 " was originally suppose to be a small part of a section, but I decided to make it a section on its own. The interview with Lola designer Bruce Ashmore is particularly insightful.

The team profile section has been expanded, with interviews designed to uncover different aspects of the Indy car racing business.

In my usual style, I reject the traditional, often diluted way of writing about the sport to present details that I'm sure you will find fascinating.

This book is guaranteed to please the new race fan, as well as the seasoned veteran.

**This book is dedicated to the memory of
Billy Vukovich III**

Table of Contents

What Does It Cost To Do Indy ?

The Indianapolis Motor Speedway on race day,1990 (IMS - Dave Willowghby photo)

Over the past few years, I have come across several articles that have attempted to determine   "What it costs to do Indy". These writings presented a basic idea about what it costs to run a car and a team at Indianapolis. Until now, a detailed account has never been documented. Some team owners make cost estimates public, but you must be aware that some owners like to exaggerate their costs in an effort to gain more sponsorship income. By writing this section, I will record what it costs to run a medium one car team for the 1991 Indianapolis 500; single meaning that we only have one driver.

Before we start, separate logistics files will be set up to keep all expenses in their proper order. These files will be as follows: car and engine expenses, travel expenses, salaries, garage expenses, and the race income. To give this section a somewhat happy ending, our driver will "make the show".

For this section, we will be renting what equipment we can and buying and reselling it after the month. We will assume that all of our crew members have jobs (and understanding bosses!) during the rest of the year, and will be taking the month off to work for our team. All of our crew members have previous experience in the Indy car field and still work in the motor racing industry.

A lot of Indy car teams are based in the Midwest, specifically Indianapolis. It would be a lot easier to rent the equipment from an Indy-based team. However, that   will assume that the equipment we need is that would be too easy.   All of our equipment will originate in Los Angeles, California. Since we only have one driver, we will only need to enter two cars for the race. Some of the larger teams such as; Penske, Galles-Kraco, or Newman-Haas, enter up to three cars for each driver. On the smaller side, some teams that only have one driver only enter one car.

Before we leave from L.A., we will be renting a complete transporter, with pit equipment from a currently defunct team. The transporter and pit equipment has been rented for six weeks for $20,000. This figure is courtesy of Lee Kunzman, team manager of Hemelgarn Racing.

Car File

For the running of the 75th Indianapolis 500, our team will be using a 1990 Lola / Buick combination. A 1991 Lola would certainly be ideal, but it wouldn't be financially feasable to buy a brand new car for only one race . Not only would a 1991 model depreciate about $140,000 after the month, orders for the 1991 Lola began in May of 1990. Since our team did not exist in 1990, our team would be at the bottom of the priority list meaning a late delivery time.

Renting cars from other teams is a rare practice, especially since we will be converting them from Chevrolet or Cosworth power over to the Buick engine.   In the fall of 1990, a used 1990 Lola with assorted spares was priced around $125,000 to $150,000. This price range is about a 35 to 47 percent depreciation from its original price of $235,000.

Our team has agreed to purchase two 1990 Lolas at $125,000 each.   We will use the lower figure since we will be buying two cars at once. The cars come complete with wheels, spare front and rear wings, electronics, shocks and springs, a spare undertray and various suspension pieces.

About the only drawback to running the Buick engine at Indy is that once a car is converted over to Buick power, it loses even more of its resale value. The reason for this is because running a Buick during the rest of the season would be uncompetitive with CART's 45 inch rule. This means that a team would have to re-convert the car over to say, Cosworth power for the rest of the 1991 season.

If both cars make it through the month without hitting any walls, we will assume that we can sell them for around $75,000 to $85,000 in June of 1991. We will have both cars painted in L.A., in April 1991. A two color paint scheme with custom computer made sponsor decals will cost $3,250 per car.

We could consider taking out an insurance policy against crash damage for our cars, however the premiums would be just about as much as the value of a car to insure for the entire month. Some teams that rent a ride on a one race basis insure their cars from race to race. However, owners that have insured their cars in the past from companies such as Lloyds, claim that it does not pay off in the long run. In fact, just as your premiums might be raised after an accident on the highway, companies that insure Indy cars also raise an owner's premiums after his car has been damaged

```
┌─────────────────────────────────────────┐
│                                         │
│              Car File                   │
│                                         │
│   2 Complete 1990 Lola chassis, with five│
│   sets of wheels and assorted spares:   │
│                                         │
│              $ 250,000                   │
│                                         │
│   Services to repaint both cars in a two│
│   color paint scheme, plus create custom│
│   sponsorship decals:                   │
│                                         │
│              $ 6,500                     │
│                                         │
│                                         │
│              Total:                      │
│                                         │
│              $ 256,500                   │
│                                         │
└─────────────────────────────────────────┘
```

Engine File

During the month of May we will be rotating a total of four Buick engines. Buick will be our engine of choice for several reasons: not only is the Buick relatively low in price a $62,500, engine rebuilds are a low $8,000 each. A Chevrolet engine might be best to have, but

let's look at it realistically. In the first place, you cannot rent Chevrolet engines. Secondly, with the extra advantage that USAC gives the Buick engine in the form of 10 extra inches of boost, the Buick has around 150 extra horsepower at Indianapolis.

The new generation Cosworth DFS could be considered, but it's a lot more expensive at $92,000 with engine rebuilds at $18 to $20,000. Basically, the Cosworth is for teams who want to run the entire year, but can't get a Chevrolet engine contract.

Buick, or any team owners or engine builders generally do not rent engines for one race only. Due to this, we must also buy our engines and turbochargers. We could buy brand new engines, but this wouldn't really be a good business move. The problem is that just like the cars, the Buick engine will lose around 40 to 50 percent of its resale value after the month of May. The reason why these engines lose so much value after Indianapolis is because they are not competitive with CART's 45 inch rule. Another problem is that an owner doesn't know if the engine rules will remain the same for another year.

Our team will be purchasing a total of four, one year old Buick engines. After all, losing a total of about $48,000 on engine depreciation sounds better than losing around $100,000 if we bought new engines. We could consider buying even older engines, but then we would lose competitiveness.

A used, one year old Buick engine has been estimated by Lee Kunzman to be worth around $30,000. Since we will be buying four at a time, and are naturally astute business people, we have talked the previous owner down to $100,000 for all four engines. These engines come complete with electronics, fuel and oil pumps, alternator, wiring loom, turbo log and flywheel.

Engine headers normally come with a new car. However since we bought used cars that had Chevy or Cosworth power to begin with, we will have to buy two brand new sets of headers. A new set of headers for the Buick will cost $8,000 per set. The reason why these are so expensive is because the pipes are custom built around the cars sidepods and undertray. We did consider buying used headers, but found that we were out of luck since no team ran a 1990 Lola/ Buick combination during the 1990 season.

We will also be needing a minimum of two clutch assemblies. Tilton engineering in California sells a regular clutch for $800. Tilton also produces a light-weight carbon / carbon clutch for $4,500 each. However, our team is not that financially courageous. Besides the carbon / carbon clutch is best used on road courses. We will also be needing a minimum of two turbo chargers. A new turbo for a Buick costs $3,500 each. During the month, we will assume that we will not blow any engines. We will, however, be blowing a turbo, meaning that we will be buying a third turbocharger by the end of the month. After Indy, we will sell the entire package to separate buyers for a total of $80,000. This is only about 30 percent depreciation, but since we are selling to separate buyers the price per engine unit will be a little more expensive.

Engine File

4 used Buick engines with support equipment:
$ 100,000

3 Turbo Chargers:
$ 10,500

2 Sets of headers:
$ 16,000

2 Clutches:
$ 1,600

Total:

$ 128,100

Salary File

Our crew will consist of seven people, plus a truck driver who will only work a limited schedule. We will be paying our crew what we think is a fair salary for the month. Since this is a medium effort, our chief mechanic and team owner will share the responsibility of team manager. The chief mechanic will also asist in the engineering set-up of the cars, so we will not need a full time engineer.

The chief mechanic's salary will be $5,000 for the month, plus 2 percent of the prize money. Our second mechanic will be paid $3,000 plus 1 percent of the prize money. The transmission man will be paid $ 3,500 plus 1 percent of the prize money. Transmission builders generally command higher salaries because they are specialists, therefore they usually have more experience than a second mechanic. Our chief mechanic knows of a few Indianapolis based people who will serve as our helpers. We will hire three helpers or "gofers" of $1,800 each for the month. One of our helper's wives will serve as our timer/scorer and receive $1,000. None of our helpers will be paid a percentage of the purse.

We will need to hire a truck driver to haul the transporter from Los Angeles to Indianapolis, then back to Los Angeles at the end of the month, but we will consider this a travel expense.

Finally, our chief, second and transmission mechanics will all be paid $25 a day per diem for meal expenses. Since our helpers all live in Indianapolis,

and therefore are not on the road, they will not receive a per diem. Part of our driver's contract specified that he will receive a per diem. A driver's per diem is generally the same as the crew's.

This leaves us with a total of four people that will require a per diem. Our crew and driver will be on the road from Thursday, May 2nd until Wednesday May 29th , for a total of 27 days of per diem at $ 25 per day. This adds up to a total of $ 2,700.

Salary File

Chief mechanic / Team manager:
$ 5,000

Second mechanic:
$ 3,000

Transmission man:
$ 3,500

3 Helpers / "Gofers" Total:
$ 5,400

Timer / Scorer:
$ 1,000

Per Diem Total:
$ 2,700

Total:
$ 20,600

Travel / Hotel File:

Since our crew lives in different parts of the country, our travel itinerary can become a little complicated. All of our airline reservations have been booked well in advance in order to get the lowest rates. From Los Angeles, the owner, his wife, driver and chief mechanic will be departing late Thursday, May 2 nd. A total of four non-refundable, business class, round trip tickets will cost $ 329 each. Our transmission man lives in Phoenix, Arizona, same departure date, $ 284 round trip. The second mechanic lives in Dallas, Texas, same departure date, $ 259 round trip. To air freight the second and transmission mechanic's tool boxes to and from Indianapolis will cost $ 125 from Phoenix and $ 100 from Dallas. Our helpers /"gofers" are all from Indianapolis, therefore require no travel arrangements.

We will be using a retired truck driver from Los Angeles to drive the transporter to Indianapolis. Our driver will leave Los Angeles on Sunday, April 28. The driver's salary will be .25 cents per mile, plus $25 per day, per diem. The trip from L.A. to Indy is 2,074 miles. After returning to L.A. at the end of the month, the driver will earn $ 1037, plus $ 200 per diem for a total of eight days on the road. The driver will then fly back to L.A. and return to Indy at the end of the month to drive the transporter back to L.A..

We will assume that the transporter has all of the proper highway permits and registration. The round trip total mileage from Los Angeles is 4,148 miles. Figuring the transporter's fuel mileage is five miles per gallon, that amounts to 830 gallons of diesel fuel. Using a national average of $1.25 per gallon, our total fuel bill is $ 1,037.

Once our team arrives in Indianapolis, we will be needing a total of three rental cars. The lowest rate we could find is $450 per car for 28 days with unlimited mileage. Our driver will be receiving a free loaner car from Stuart Skillman Oldsmobile in Indianapolis. Stuart Skillman annually provides vehicles for all drivers who have made the race in the previous year. GMC corporation provides vehicles for all CART teams, however our team will not participate in any CART races so these vehicles are unavailable to our team.

Our team will rent apartments about five minutes from the track. We will be renting a one bedroom unit for the owner and his wife, a one bedroom unit for our driver, (which was specified in his contract), and two, two-bedroom units for the chief, second and transmission mehanics. The two-bedroom units will cost $ 1,150 each and the one bedroom units will cost $1,050 each. These rooms are all furnished with maid service. In addition, each apartment will require a $ 200 security deposit.

These figures are an average around the city of Speedway, Indiana during the month of May. Of course, each complex raises its rates dramatically if you are only renting for the month of May only. In fact, the complex can raise its rates by up to 100 percent for this month only. If we were to stay at a hotel, we could expect to pay up to twice as much as the above rates.

Travel / Hotel File

Airline ticket total:
$ 2,188
Rental car total:
$ 1,350
Apartment total:
$ 5,200
Truck driver salary total:
$ 1,237
Fuel for transporter:
$ 1,037
Toolbox air freight:
$ 225

Total:
$ 11,237

Garage / Pit File

Garage and pit expenses are probably the most overlooked item when it comes to adding up a team budget. First of all, we will need to rent the traditional parts washer and shop rags. Parts washer service for the month will run $ 200. Shop rags, towels and carpets will cost around $ 750. To power all of the air tools and pit equipment, we will spend a minimum of $400 on nitrogen bottles.

Since this is the modern era, we would also like to rent some furniture for the garage. Nothing too fancy, just a small sofa and a table and chairs. Old- timers tend to look into today's garages in Gasoline Alley, see plush furniture and shake their heads. Well, when you have a $ 300,000 sponsor come to visit your garage, it's pretty tacky to have them sit on a five gallon bucket of Valvoline. Furniture and a refrigerator will cost around $ 175 to rent for the month. To stock the refrigerator with soda, candy and other goodies, add another $ 200 for the month.

Dry cleaning for all of our crew and driver uniforms will cost as high as $ 1,200 for the month. If you figure that we have seven crewman, plus the owner and his wife, that makes nine sets of shirts and pants per day, multiply this by 27 days, this equals 243 crew items to be cleaned during the month. The driver will need his suit cleaned after each day of practice. If he drives the full 18 days of running possible, that's at least $ 200 alone. $ 1,200 for dry cleaning is a good figure for a small to medium team. The larger teams such as Penske Racing, can spend as much as $3,500 for dry cleaning for the month. Thinking of opening a dry cleaning shop in Indianapolis? Telephone and long distance service will amount to at least $ 1,000. This is a conservative estimate from owner Dale Coyne.

All of the motor oil, brake cleaner, grease, hand soap and spray lubricants are compliments of Valvoline. Valvoline also provides free Methanol for all teams using their motor oil. All of our nut and bolt needs will be courtesy of Premier Corporation.

We will also include the tire bill in this file. Of course, we will be using Goodyear tires. The average team in 1990 used 25 sets of tires during the month. The fronts cost $181 each, the rears cost $255 each. At $ 872 per set, multiplied by 25 sets, our tire bill will be $21,800.

Garage / Pit File

Shop Rags / Carpets:
$ 800
Parts Washer Service:
$ 250

Nitrogen Bottle Service:
$ 300

Furniture / Refrigerator Rental:
$ 175

Groceries:
$ 200

Dry Cleaning:
$ 1,200

Telephone:
$ 1,000

Tires:
$ 21,800

Total:

$ 25,725

Miscellaneous Expenses

Before we end our expense records, there are several costs that do not fit into any particular catagory.

Entry fees for the Indianapolis 500 is $ 3,000 per car, plus $ 1,000 deposit per garage. With each entry you get one garage, pit badges and tickets to the awards banquet at the end of the month. It will cost $ 8,000 to enter both cars plus deposits.

Each of our crew members are also required to join USAC. The team owner always pays this expense. A one year membership costs $ 100 per person, $ 250 each for the owner, driver and chief mechanic. This will cost the team a total of $ 1,350.

Each team is also required to provide its own liability insurance. This insurance is designed to protect the owner in case a spectator is injured or killed as a result of an incident involving our car.

Example: In 1987, a right front wheel came off of Tony Bettenhausen's car during the race, in turn three. The wheel bounced off of the nose of Roberto Guerrero's car, then flew into the crowd and killed one spectator. That spectator's family sued every party that they could, and the matter was settled out of court.

K&K Insurance located in Fort Wayne, Indiana insures around 85 percent of the motor racing industry in North America. A five million dollar policy will cost our team $1,000 for the month. We must also insure the team's golf cart while it is in or around Gasoline Alley. Add another $300 for golf cart insurance.

All of our crew members and driver are covered by USAC and the Indianapolis Motor Speedway Corporation in case of injury or death.

Crew uniforms come in all sorts of colors and price ranges. If our team was doing the entire season, we could spend as much as $200 per uniform including pants, shirts and custom embroidering. Embroidering can cost up to $100 per shirt. Since we are only doing Indy, we really don't want to spend that much. On the other hand, we don't want our crew to look like a bunch of bums! Polo shirts with our sponsors name in small embroidery would go along great with Levi's cotton Docker slacks. Lets figure $100 per shirt/pant set. Clothing a total of eight crew men, including the owner, multiplied by three sets of uniforms per person, leaves a total of $2,400.

Our driver will be wearing Simpson safety equipment. Simpson provides drivers with free helmets and fire retardent underwear. The driver's suits will be paid for by Goodyear in exchange for their logo to be displayed on the uniforms. The average driver rotates four uniforms per season.

Since we rented the transporter complete with pit equipment and older crew uniforms from the previous team, most of our crew members have found fire retardant uniforms to fit them on race day. However, we must purchase additional uniforms for our crew. It's a financial shame that uniforms can not be rented from Simpson or Bell for race day only, but that's the way it is. Every May, before the race, several teams flock to these uniform makers and ask to rent uniforms for their people. Not even the television networks are immune to this disorganization. The reason why uniform makers do not rent these fire suits is because they are custom fit to several body measurements.

We have discovered that we need suits for three of our crew members, plus five pairs of shoes. A Simpson one layer suit costs $ 284 each. High-top fire retardent shoes cost $ 109 per pair. We will assume that there is enough fire retardant underwear, gloves and refueling helmets to go around. The total for the fire suits and shoes is $ 1,288.

Since our chief, second and transmission mechanics are the only qualified "over the wall" pit crew on race day, we will need to hire two additional tire changers and one vent man.

Former crew men who live in Indianapolis regularly sell their services to race teams for race day only. The going rate is $ 500 per man. These race day only crew men will receive no percentage of the purse. One of our helpers will do the pit board, the others will help with the tires and hoses behind the pit wall.

Finally, it would be nice to invite our sponsors to a round of golf in the Speedway Golf Tournament. After all, golf is the international game of business. If four of the top executives of our sponsoring company play in the tournament, plus the car owner, driver and chief mechanic, at $ 50 per player, add another $ 350 for " field " expenses.

It would also be a nice gesture to purchase the official qualifying photo of our car and driver for our sponsors sales representatives. 100 8 x 10 color photos will cost a total of $ 500 from the Indianapolis Motor Speedway photo shop.

As a souvenier of his trip to the 1991 Indianapolis 500, we could also present an original brick from the old racing surface to the chaiman of the board of our sponsoring company. Let's say that we bought one from a local collector for $ 200.

Miscellaneous Expenses

Entry Fee / Deposit:
$ 8,000

USAC Registration:
$ 1,350

Liability Insurance:
$ 1,350

Crew Uniforms:
$ 2,400

Race Day Crew men:
$ 1,500

Golf / Photos / Original Brick:
$ 1,050

Total:

$ 15,650

Crash Damage

Since I am trying to make this demonstration as real as possible, our budget will also include a moderate crash. Chances of crashing vary widely, however the month might be too easy for our crew if our driver did not find the third turn wall without injury.

Let's say that our driver got up into the gray stuff in turn three, hit the wall with the right side of the car, then slid into the infield with no further contact.

We do have a backup car to use in the mean time, but since the crash was before we qualified, we need the other car as soon as possible. After all, what happens if the backup car is wrecked ?

We will assume that the car can be repaired with the following damage:

The right side pod and undertray can be repaired. The right front and rear suspension needs to be replaced, including wishbones, uprights and brakes. We will also need a new oil cooler and ignition box.

Probably the most time consuming repair will be where the front suspension wishbones came back and punctured a hole in the tub. If a tub is severely damaged, the car is considered to be totaled. If the tub is moderately damaged it can be shipped back to Lola Cars in England for repairs. Since our tub is only lightly damaged, and we need it repaired as soon as possible, it can be repaired locally. Carbon fiber and aluminum honeycomb repair is performed by a combination of Eloisa Garza and Jack Howerton. Both have shops just a few miles south of the Speedway. To repair a small to moderate hole in the side of a tub is estimated to cost from $ 3,000 to $ 8,000. Our repair will cost $ 6,000.

Repairs to the side pod and undertray will cost $8,000. A brand new under tray alone costs $ 20,000 for a 1990 Lola. You may remember that we have a spare undertray, but it was designed for road course races. Since we do have spare wings and various suspension pieces, the financial damage is minimized. If we did have to buy brand new front and right rear suspension, uprights and brakes, that would cost around $ 25,000. Uprights alone cost around $ 6,000 each! Let's say that we will only need to buy $ 5,000 worth of suspension. Among the other pieces that we brought back on the wrecker were the spark (ignition) box and the oil cooler. Spark boxes cost $1,000. An oil cooler (radiator) costs another $2,000. If you think that paying $6,000 for a single upright (wheel assembly) and $2,000 for a 16 x 20 inch oil cooler is a bit ridiculous, then welcome to the wonderful world of big time motor racing ! We must also repace the right engine header, which will cost a mere $ 4,000.

Finally, the car needs some paint attention. The right side pod and engine cover must be totally repainted The tub can be spot painted. Paint damage will cost $1,500.

If you think painting an Indy car is too expensive, this is why; carbon fiber has a rough texture and to properly fill this surface requires a lot of time and skill. If you simply fill the surface with paint to make it smooth, it adds too much weight to the car.

```
┌─────────────────────────────────┐
│         Crash Damage            │
│                                 │
│         Tub Repair:             │
│          $ 6,000                │
│                                 │
│   Side Pod / Undertray Repair:  │
│          $ 8,000                │
│                                 │
│      Suspension Repair:         │
│          $ 5,000                │
│                                 │
│         Oil Cooler:             │
│          $ 2,000                │
│                                 │
│         Spark Box:              │
│          $ 1,000                │
│                                 │
│       Engine Header:            │
│          $ 4,000                │
│                                 │
│      Repaint Bodywork:          │
│          $ 1,500                │
│                                 │
│           Total:                │
│          $ 27,500               │
└─────────────────────────────────┘
```

$142,384 minus 10 percent equals $14,238, leaving us with $142, 384. 1. 2 percent of this equals $1,538, leaving $126,608.

The driver and respective crew receive their share based on $126,608. The driver's share of 40 percent comes to $50,643. The chief mechanic's share of 2 percent equates to $2,532. The second and transmission mechanics share of 1 percent is $1,266 each. The driver's and crew's share of the purse equals $55,707.

This leaves our team with a final total of $70,901 for finishing 11th in the 1991 Indianapolis 500.

```
┌─────────────────────────────────┐
│           The Race              │
│                                 │
│      Total Prize Money:         │
│          $ 142,384              │
│                                 │
│     Less USAC / State Tax:      │
│          $ 15,776               │
│                                 │
│      Driver's Percentage:       │
│          $ 50,643               │
│                                 │
│      Crew's Percentage:         │
│          $ 5,064                │
│                                 │
│      Car Owner's Total:         │
│          $ 70,901               │
└─────────────────────────────────┘
```

The Race

Through the luck of the draw, our driver will finish 11th in the race. I have determined this finishing position by drawing numbers out of a hat. Since this demonstration was written in December 1990, we will use the 1990 Indianapolis prize money as an example. 11th place paid a total of $142,384. Our driver was contracted at 50 percent of the prize money if he finished 1st thru 3rd, 40 percent for positions 4th thru 33rd. These percentages are the going rate.

Before our driver and team gets its share of the prize money, certain percentages are taken off the top. First of all, USAC takes 10 percent off of the top of all finishing positions. This 10 percent is to cover the sanctioning bodies administrative expenses and the USAC Gold Crown Championship. After that, the state of Indiana deducts a 1.2 percent state gross tax.

Now that all of our expenses have been documented, it's time to add everything up and compare the costs to the winnings. Before we do this, let's remember that we will sell the cars and the engines at the end of the month to several buyers.

The two cars with spares and wheels have a total resale value of $ 150,000. The four engines with support equipment have a total resale value of $80,000.

You may have noticed that the figure of $ 150,000 for both cars is $ 10,000 lower than our original estimate of $ 160,000. This $ 10,000 loss is due to the crash damage to one of the cars. Although the car was completely repaired, once a car has crashed it loses some of its performance capability, therefore losing its resale appeal. We will also be getting back our deposits for the garage and apartments. The garage deposit was $2,000, while the apartment deposits totalled $800.

File Total	
Transporter Rental:	$ 20,000
Cars:	$ 256,000
Engines:	$ 128,100
Salaries:	$ 20,600
Travel / Lodging:	$ 11,262
Garage / Pit:	$ 25,725
Miscellaneous:	$ 15,650
Crash Repair:	$ 27,500
File Total:	$ 503,837
Race Income:	$ 70,901
Resale Income From Cars:	$ 150,000
Resale Income From Engines:	$ 80,000
Less Deposits Paid Back:	$2,800
Owner's Net Cost:	$190,136

So now you know what it costs to do Indy. You could sit back and throw all kinds of variables into these costs, but that's really out of the owner's control. We could say that we finished first in the race and received over 1.2 million dollars in prize money, but let's face it, that really wouldn't happen to a medium team like ours.

We could figure on no crash damage. On the other hand, we could figure on crashing both cars and missing the race altogether. That cruel predicament happened to Stoops Racing in 1990.

The last figure will be the all mighty sponsorship dollar. It will cost our team $190,136 to do Indy. So our owner needs this amount in sponsorship to break even. The good news is that sponsorship for a medium team for Indianapolis only averages somewhere between $300,000 to $500,000. Taking the middle figure of $ 400,000, lets see how much money our owner made.

Since our sponsor was found through a public relations agent, There is a 15 percent commission which is paid to the lucky soul who inked the contract first. That means that if we had $400,000 worth of sponsors, the PR agent would receive a $60,000 commission, leaving the owner with only $340,000 Using this figure, the owner made a profit of $ 169,864. Considering the effort involved, this would be a nice profit. On the other hand, look at how much money the owner has to put up and risk.

Perhaps the bottom line is that team owners are in this business to make money. However, to hear these owners talk, you would swear that they are always losing money. The reason why is because team owners never consider how much sponsorship income they are receiving. The average Indy car owner would probably rather visit the dentist rather than reveal his exact sponsorship income.

We have now learned that Indy car racing is a business. If an owner does happen to lose money, he can always write it off his tax bill. The reason I say bill is because most of the Indy car owners are multi-millionaires. If you are a multi-millionaire, then you probably have great business sense. Losing money on an Indy car team defies all good business sense. After all, nobody starts a business for the sole purpose of creating tax write-offs. Fortunately, our owner will probably be writing a healthy check to the I.R.S. from his extra income for his Indy car effort.

As an extra bonus for the month, the team will be awarded 11th place prize money for the USAC Gold Crown Championship. This championship consists of the running of the Indianapolis 500 only. Only the top 24 finishing positions receive this prize money. Our prize will amount to $12,814, which is paid in February of the following year-- in our case, February 1992. Our driver will receive his 40 percent ($5,126) and the owner will get the remaining $7,688.

Who knows, the owner just might use his earnings as the first step to run a team for the 1992 running of the Indianapolis 500.

The author would like to thank Dale Coyne and Lee Kunzman for their help in compiling this information.

One-On-One With Rick Mears

In 1978, Roger Penske hired a young driver by the name of Rick Mears. In the early days, some critics, mostly through jealousy, were curious why Penske would hire such a young driver to team with his veteran, "hot shoe" drivers. Over the decade of the 80's, Rick Mears became a legend. With all of Rick's accomplishments, as well as hard times, I thought that it would be a good time to sit down and talk about the many happenings that have occurred over the past 13 years. A lot of writers merely cover the sugary, packaged side of drivers. I wanted to capture a different side of perhaps the nicest, down to earth drivers on the circuit.

Rick Amabile: How many hours per week would you say you spend with your sponsorship commitments, both during and off season ?

Rick Mears: I've never really kept track of it, and it varies so much. During the season at different races, depending on the area and how heavy a sponsor wants to work you on certain areas, certain races are better for them than others. You work a lot heavier at one particular track, one particular race, than they will at some of the others. Some of them are pretty light, so it just depends. The heavy ones, you come in a day or two ahead of time, whether it's going to a mall or going to one of their dealer's places, like a store, whatever the case may be, signing autographs or getting together at a dinner with their dealers, it just varies a lot. I've never really kept track of the time.

Amabile: Is there a lot more during the off-season ?

Mears: No, not really, again that varies. Myself, being with Pennzoil for so long, I never really got to see how other types of sponsors work. Depending on the product and your sponsor, they work a different way, if a sponsor is public orientated....like Gould Electronics. When I first started with Penske, they weren't really a public orientated company. They didn't have dealers, it was just something that they were looking for a name recognition. Since they didn't have dealers or anything, they didn't do much in the way of commercials. I'd go to the plants once in a while all over the country and go through and meet all of the people in the plant. We didn't do much in the way of storesor anything like that. With Pennzoil , whether it's Kroger, K-Mart, G.I. Joes, whatever the store may be, that may be a big dealer of theirs in a certain area, then you go and work the stores. I go to their stores to help draw people in that way, they all work a little bit different. I've been with Pennzoil most of the time, so that's really the only one that I can speak for.

Amabile: Has anything really funny happened when you do in-store appearances, like somebody wanting to meet you so bad or whatever ?

Mears: Oh yeah, that takes place. It makes you feel good, it makes you feel fortunate to be in that position. I can't really think of a specific instance. Sometimes I'll run into a relation that I didn't know I had, you know, someone will come up and say "we've got to be a cousin from way back", that kind of thing. There are so many of them that I draw a blank on any one example. You get some funny stuff quite a bit. It's amazing too, I'll run into some people, the same people, at a lot of different places. They follow the circuit, and happen to be in the area, they hear that you're going to be at a certain store and they show up to see you. I'll see the same person at five different races. It's fun.

Amabile: What's it like when you crank on the ol tube and you see yourself on a T.V. commercial ? Do you just feel real flattered ?

Mears: I feel flattered, but I feel terrible too. Usually the performance is not that well (laughing). I don't think I've ever been happy with anything I've ever done. There's some that are better than others, there's some that I feel...well, that's not that bad. I pick it apart. I'm my worst critic. Once I see it finished and look at it, you don't get much of an opportunity to watch it while you're doing it. You don't really know how it's coming off. You have to take the directors word for it. The director can make all the difference. Different directors are really good at being able to draw out what they want. It's like anything else, if you're happy with 75 percent, then that's what you're going to get. If you're not, then you work to get 90 or 100 percent. Some directors will keep it up and learn the person that they're working with. If I could watch each deal that I did and kind of critique it, then I'd be going back and saying, no let's do it over and let's do it over again and again. I'd be worse then they are, until we finally got it right. What I think looks right may not neccessarily be what they are trying to accomplish. There's a lot of variables there.

After 8 sucessful years with Pennzoil, Mears and Penske will have to look down the pit lane to see their once familiar colors. (Doug Wendt photo)

Amable: How hard is it to create free time for yourself, both during and off season ?

Mears: It's difficult. The past five years, the series has grown so much.... I mean I always thought that it was hectic from day one, compared to what I was used to.

Amable: Day one meaning before you first won Indy?

Mears: Yeah, that normal lifestyle. I was just used to going to work every day, eight hours a day, then go home. There's no such thing as an eight hour day anymore.

Amable: What did you do before you started driving full time ?

Mears: I was in constuction. I worked for my dad.

Amable: As a back-hoe driver ?

Mears: Yeah, back-hoe and equipment driver. I've dug a lot of ditches! (laughing)

Amable: Do you ever go back and mess around with it ?

Mears: I haven't for a long time. Some time ago I bought a house in Bakersfield, and it had been quite a while since I had been on a hoe and I wanted to build a block fence around my house. In order to save a little money, I thought I'd dig the footing myself. So I called dad up and said I was coming over to borrow the hoe. So I ran over and grabbed the hoe and went back over to my house and started digging the footings. After about 30 feet of digging the footings, I thought my fingers were going to fall off ! I hadn't worked my fingers in a long time, so I had to start over again. It's like riding a bicycle, once you get back on it you're a little bit rusty.

Amable: At least you didn't hit any water pipes !

Mears: Right, but I have done that in my time !

Amable: When you meet people, what's the biggest misconception about race drivers that people ask, both sponsors and fans ?

Mears: I think for me, and different drivers are different, myself, everybody thinks that I am a risk taker, that I'm a daredevil. Everyone thinks that I like to take chances and that kind of thing, but I don't, I never have. When I tell people that they look at me like " yeah right" ! I've always wanted to keep everything as calculated as possible. To me, it's not taking a risk unless you're out of your element. If you're out of your element and you're into something that you don't know, and you start taking big steps instead of small steps just to sneak up onto it, then it gets risky. If you take your time and do it a little bit at a time, take it at your own pace, what feels right to you and to the equipment, then it's not that risky. Some of the other guys become more of the risk, because you don't know what they're going to do. So in that respect it gets risky. If all I had to do is rely on what I do, then I don't feel that it's risky. When you start calculating in everybody else....tire failure and stuff like that, then those parts that you have no control over become the risk, that's one of the biggest things. People think that you're a speed demon, speed has nothing to do with it. That's probably one of the biggest misconceptions right there. Everybody thinks that you love speed, that you love going fast, and that's not the case. What it boils down to, for me is just going a little faster than the next guy. If everybodys running 30, I want to run 31. If everybody's running 230, I want to run 231. So it's the competition, not the speed or the risk.

Amable: Do you see any difference between rookie drivers now, from maybe ten years ago ?

Mears: It's varied over the years. You've always had a wide range of rookies. I'd say early on....you maybe had a little bit better rookie selection, but it was because at that point in time you couldn't rent a ride. You worked your way into it more, on your ability. Then that kind of went by the wayside, and got to a point where anybody that had enough money in their pocket could rent a ride and get a ride. There was a stretch in between where the quality was maybe not as good. You had good ones, but then there were quite a few that weren't. But now it seems like it's kind of worked its way back. That's part of the business now, is learning to get in and promote yourself, drum up sponsorship and help out in that respect, that's part of the industry. I think that it's so competitive today that you've got to be able to do both. Before you didn't necessarily have to be able to promote or drive, if you had the money in your pocket you could get something together. Now, you've got to be able to do it all because it's so competitive. You're going to be in the public eye quite a bit because we have so much more recognition today then we used to. A lot more corporate people are involved, so you have to be able to hold up that end, yet you have to be competitive. It's tough. It's a very tight deal. You've got a lot of cars, good cars, good equipment and good teams. It doesn't matter about the money that much, you've got to be able to go out there and hold up your own. So I think that it's worked it's way back a little bit. The rookies that are coming in have very good abilities.

Amable: Okay, here's a touchy one. I'm not going to mention any names, but there are some drivers out there still that come up with a big chunk of money and their ability is sort of questionable. Do any of the top drivers ever go to CART or USAC or the Speedway and say " you've got to be serious, this guy's a joke"? I mean, it's your ass out there that's racing with them.

Mears: Yeah, it has a little bit in the past from time to time. There's been things said. You know, you say hey, you guys need to take a closer look here, keep your eye on them, that kind of thing. It has come up, yes.

Amable: When you're in Bakersfield or your second home in Florida, everywhere you go, are you always recognized by people, like if you go to a store or something ?

Mears: It depends. There's times that you are and there's times where it's fairly quiet. A lot of it depends on your past season. If you had a good season, you're recognizable (laughing). If you didn't, then it's a little quieter. It depends where you're at. Around Indianapolis, obviously the month of May, you can't go out of the door without it. Everyone knows that the drivers are in town. People see the name or the face on T.V. and the news everyday. So you're much more recognizable there and obviously in your home town you get quite a bit of it there. It surprises me that in Florida, I almost get recognized as much as I do in California. I just feel real fortunate. I'll see people, a lot of people, all over the country, in traveling that recognize me, but then you see a lot of people that look at me ....and I can tell that they recognize me, but they can't put two and two together. If you don't have a racing jacket or a racing hat on, then they don't make the connection. I'll walk by someone and they glance over and they kind of nod like they know you, and they know they've seen you before somewhere, but they can't place where at. If you're a Paul Newman or somebody like that where it's absolutely household, then you can't go anywhere. We're fortunate in that respect. The majority of the time people see us with our fire suits on and a helmet in a race car. When you do get away, they don't pick up quite as quick.

Amabile: When you're in Indy, when you check into a hotel, do you have to use assumed name ? You know, like movie or rock stars, so people can't bother you ?

Mears: No, I don't do that. It would probably be easier at times, but I don't worry about it. If it gets too hectic, then you make arrangements to try to slow it down.

Amabile: During the month of May, do you have to send your wife out to do everything ?

Mears: At times, yes. We have a lot of room service! (laughing) Because it's tough for us to go out to a restaurant.

Amabile: The guy comes to the door and has your meal and then he wants your autogragh too . (laughing).

Mears: Oh yeah, that's standard. You don't worry about that, that kind of thing happens full time.

Amabile: Do you have a favorite part about being well known ?

Mears: ....Well, it's a good feeling to have people support you and be behind you. It's a very good feeling.... and satisfying. A favorite part.....I don't know off hand.

Amabile: What business interests do you have ?

Mears: I really have not gotten involved in a lot of things. Again, here's the no-risk factor coming in. There's a lot of things out there that I can get involved with, there's a lot of people knocking on the door saying, you know, " I've got a hell of a deal here for you". I decided a long time ago that, and it's my nature, I don't like taking a chance. I've always taken the conservative approach. To me, being conservative is putting it away somewhere and letting it draw interest. When I get enough together to play with, then I'll play a little with some of it. I'll never play with an amount that

I think will take food off of the table, so to speak. I'm involved with with the Penske (Cadillac) dealership in Bakersfield, but I'm just a small part, Penske is the major. I have some property in Bakersfield. Industrial property, rental for small businesses, leasing, something that takes care of itself. I'm involved with Victory Lane quick lube centers, they 're mainly on the east coast, I've been their spokesman for quite a few years.

Amabile: I remember watching in the early 80's, where they were all saying that you were going to do Formula One racing, what ever happened to that ?

Mears: I just decided against it, when all that started coming about. I've always enjoyed driving different things, getting into different cars, just the mystique, the wondering if I could do it attitude. You know, are these guys supermen or not. The first thing that I found out in Indy cars is that there are no supermen. Everybody puts their pants on one leg at a time. It's a matter of making the right decision at the right time, the right equipment, trying to keep your head screwed on straight. When the F-1 offer came about, it was about the time that CART and USAC were struggling, and I didn't know what was going to happen. I didn't know if CART was going to go, or USAC was going to go, or what the case was going to be. So I had the opportunity to drive the Brabham car. I talked to Bernie Ecclestone and he wanted me to drive for him. I was curious about the F-1 car, curious about how they run and their drivers and everything. So I went and did a couple tests for them. That basically satisfied my curiosity. In the mean time, while I was doing the test, CART started coming together, and I didn't want to give up the Penske organization. I was very happy with the team, with Penske and the whole operation and I was fairly new, there was still a lot that I wanted to accomplish in Indy cars. I went and did the test for Brabham, I ran basically as quick as Nelson (Piquet). We did a test over at Paul Ricard (France) which was

The era when drivers could keep to themselves and not talk to many people is long gone. Here Rick takes time to address a function for the 1990 Marlboro 500.
(Schulman photo)

his home track, and I ran within about a half a second of him. That was without taking any chances, because I didn't want to make a mistake. So that really satisfied my curiousity that I could be competitive if I went and ran over there.

Amabile: When they saw you go so quick, did they make you an offer ?

Mears: Oh yeah, we came to terms on everything, we made a deal. It was just a matter of me making the final decision whether I wanted to or not. Then we did another test at Riverside (California), and I ran quicker than Nelson. We could've been in the hunt, and that was the year that he won the World Championship, his first championship. It would have been a very good opportunity had I pursued it. But I didn't want to give up the Penske organization and I liked the United States. I was happier with this organization, with this Country, with everything involved. I would have had to move my family to Europe five months out of the year, and jump back and forth across the pond. I couldn't do both. If I was going to do one, I was going to do that one only.

Amabile: Coming back from an injury, do your feet still hurt you from your crash at Sanair (Canada in 1984) ?

Mears: Every day. There's not a day where I don't feel it. I don't even try to take asprin or Bufferin anymore, it just doesn't do it.

Amabile: Is it achiness or pain or what ?

Mears: It just depends. That first ten steps every morning is a killer. When I get out of bed, I want to crawl a little while. It takes a little while to get 'em limbered up, get 'em going. When I sit on a plane, which I do so often, I can feel the pressure change, going up and down in the plane.

Amabile: You can feel it in your feet ?

Mears: Yeah. After I'm off of them, like sitting on a plane from two, four or six hours depending on the flight, my feet swell, my shoes get tight. That walk up the runway, walking off of the plane is a killer. I just have to get them going again when I'm off of them for a while. When I get back on them they hurt, I just have to limber them up.

Amabile: What about when it gets cold ?

Mears: Yeah, I can really feel it. I can feel if it's going to rain. You've heard people with broken arms or legs or bad joints say " I'm starting to ache, it feels like it's going to start raining" well it's true.

Amabile: You're 39 now. Do you still see yourself driving in like ten years from now, like Mario is still doing ?

Mears: It just depends. That's something that I can't really put a finger on. I could run for ten years, I could run for three years, I could run for five years. To me, it's going to depend on whether.... There's two things that can happen that will get me out of the car. One of them being if I no longer enjoy it. If it becomes a pain to where I don't like it, I won't do it. The reason for that is that if I don't enjoy it, I won't put out the effort that I

Rick takes time out to meet and sign an autograph for one of the CART kids during a break in practice.
(Dan Boyd photo)

should to do it right. It's like anything, if you don't enjoy it, you're not going to put out 100 percent. That's not fair, it's not fair to the sponsors, it's not fair to the team, it's not fair to Penske, if I don't put out the effort. The other would be if I physically felt that I couldn't do it the way it should be done. Whichever one happens first, then I'll get out.

Amabile: A few years ago, some teams were offering you bigger money to go and drive for them. I remember you saying that you wanted to stay with Penske, because he took care of you. Even now, if someone came to you and offered you all kinds of money, would you jump ship or stay with Penske ?

Mears: No, I'd stay with Penske. I feel that in the long run....first off, we're friends. I've always been pretty loyal to people. I feel that's the way it should be. If somebody helps you, you help them. I've always felt that this team, in the long haul, we'll have our ups and downs, any team has their high points and their low points, I always felt with this organization, you're going to have them, but they're fewer and farther between. We'll have a low point, but this team can respond and get it turned around faster than most. That's because of the way Penske is, he's competitive, he's going to do whatever it takes to get it ironed out. You don't have to be a genius to figure that out, just weigh the facts. As far as I'm concerned, there is not a better team in the business. A perfect example is the '84 win (at Indianapolis). We had the Penske and it wouldn't work.. Then Penske goes and buys a March and we end up winning the race. He wants to do whatever it takes. He wants to win as bad as we do. He'll put his pride aside, just because his name's on it. If it's not as good then he'll do away with it and put it on the shelf until we make it good enough.

Amabile: What's been the scariest accident in your career ?

Mears: Well, obviously the feet was the worst. That's the first time that I ever broke a bone. I'd raced motorcycles, buggies and everything else all my life, that was the first time I'd ever broke a bone. That was the most devastating crash I ever had. It was scary, but it was already over with by the time I had time to really get scared about it

Amabile: Were you upset with yourself after the accident ?

Mears: Yeah, it was stupid. It was a stupid move. The one that really scared me the most was the fire (at Indianapolis in 1981). That was the scariest, but the feet was the worst accident.

Amabile: Back in 1979, when you first won Indy. Your sons were like five or six years old and playing with their Hot Wheels or whatever, now they're 16 and 17, how do you feel about them becoming race car drivers ?

Mears: It's up to them. I've always felt that whatever they want to do, I'll support them. I was very fortunate to make a living at my hobby, what I liked doing. Not a lot of people get that opportunity. It made me realize that. So I've always felt that whatever they decide they want to do, and what they enjoy the most, then I'll help them in any way that I can. If it's racing, fine. If it's not, fine. I've never pushed racing on them at all, in fact, as a matter of fact, I've actually shied them away from it, to a point, because it's a tough business. If that's what they decide they want to do, and they're willing to put out a 100 percent effort and do it right, then I'll support them. Clint, my oldest one, the 17 year old, he's definitly interested. Cole, my youngest one, he's into music. He likes the guitar and the bands, the heavy metal. I want to help him, because I like music too.

Amabile: What kind of music do you listen to ?

Mears: I don't listen to any one in particular, I change around. I like easy music at times, but mainly just kind of an easy rock. I'm not up on the names, if I like a song, then I get it.

Amabile: What's it like shaking a car down for the first time ? Are you a bit nervous ?

Mears: You are, but it's fun. You're curious to see how it's going to work. If it's better or worse, or what the character of the car is, because they're all different in their mannerisms or whatever. It's fun to go out and feel a car for the first time, and see what it's like. You're a little apprehensive about it because it is all new. It's exciting and it's fun because you're curious and you 've got your fingers crossed to hope that it's going to be a very good car.

Amabile: What's the first thing you notice ? Is it the handling or the ride or the downforce ?

Mears: It just depends, it's never the same twice. This business changes all the time so you have to adapt quickly. So that's what you do, you go out and as it gives you feedback, then you respond to it. You just kind of play it by ear, all the time.

Amabile: How many miles of winter testing does Penske do all together ?

Mears: There's been years where we do quite a few more test miles than we do race miles. I've heard like three to four to five thousand miles.

Amabile: I'll bet that keeps you in shape ?

Mears: Oh yeah.

Amabile: Do you work out with weights and all that stuff ?

Mears: Yeah, from time to time depending on what time of the season. Mostly just Nautilus type equipment, because those are everywhere, I'm on the road all of the time, so it's tough to get any kind of routine going. You just have to grab it when and where you're at. Most hotels have a weight room so I hit that when and where I can. When I'm at home in in Bakersfield, I got a place where I go to. During the middle of the season, you're in the car so much, and you can work out till you're blue in the face, and you can get in the car and find out muscles that you didn't know you had. It's an isometric in the car, it's a little different. It's a constant effort, you're loaded all the time. Weights, you work with weights, you pull them, you push them, you lift them, whatever. You do repetition and that kind of thing. In the race car it's actually an isometric. You're turning, when you 're turning, you lean on it, you load everything up and you hold it all the way through the corner. On some tracks, on certain ovals, you hold a lot more effort for a longer period of time. So it's almost a continuous isometric, so it's a little bit different than lifting weights.

Amabile: Your main sponsor is Marlboro now, so you're wearing your Marlboro Challenge uniform full-time now.

Mears: Right (laughing).

Amabile: So now you have to get used to not saying Pennzoil during interviews.

Mears: That's right. The first interview I did for Marlboro, I think I said Pennzoil....no, I didn't say Pennzoil, I said Pen, Marlboro (laughing).

Amabile: Do you still talk to Sullivan very much ?

Mears: Oh yeah, we're good friends.

Amabile: Are you looking forward to working with Marlboro since you were with Pennzoil for so long ?

Mears: Yeah, they're a first class company. I've worked with them before as an associate sponsor, so I'm used to it. I'm looking forward to it.

Marlboro Penske Chevy 90

1. Gearbox oil-cooler NASA ducts
2. Rear shock cooling ducts
3. Turbo air scoop
4. Pop-off valve, air jack socket and fuel vent holes
5. Speedway radiator duct covers
6. One piece engine and side pod cover
7. Driver's seat
8. Pop-off valve
9. Airjack socket
10. Mechanical fuel pump
11. Roll-over hoop
12. Tank access panel (Refueling valve on opposite side)
13. Comfort padding
14. Rear view mirror
15. Gear shift lever
16. Quick release steering wheel
17. Left hand water radiator
18. Instrument pod
19. Front and rear swaybar adjusters
20. Front spring/shock access panel
21. Double wishbone and pushrod front suspension
22. Aerodynamic brake duct
23. Tread depth slot
24. Front radial tire, 25.5 x 9.5 - 15
25. Pedal and master cylinder access panel
26. Adjustable flap
27. Road track front wing
28. Speedway front wing
29. Crash-resistant nose
30. Carbon fiber wing pole
31. Aluminum honeycomb and carbon fiber chassis
32. Brake and clutch master cylinders and reservoirs

33. Throttle, brake and clutch pedals
34. Fire extinguisher bottle
35. Front air jacks
36. Ventilated and cross-drilled front disc brake
37. Aerodynamic cast magnesium 10" x 15" front wheel
38. Road and short oval vortex generator
39. Radiator duct
40. Right hand water radiator
41. Two-piece carbon fiber underwing
42. Electronic engine management box
43. Alternator control box
44. Delco battery
45. Underwing brace
46. Right hand closing panel
47. Underwing support
48. Exhaust header heat shield
49. Ilmor-Chevrolet turbocharged V-8 engine, 2.65 liters/161 cubic inches
50. Turbocharger inlet duct
51. Right hand waste gate
52. Underwing support
53. Double wishbone and pushrod rear suspension
54. Cast magnesium hub carrier
55. Rear wheel (14" x 15") and radial tire (27 x 14-15)
56. Four-piston rear brake caliper
57. Holset turbocharger
58. In-board rear air jacks
59. Five or six speed plus reverse Penske gearbox
60. Gearbox oil cooler duct
61. Gearshift linkage
62. Gearbox oil cooler
63. Four element road race rear wing
64. Speedway rear wing

20

When people look to the future of Indy car racing, they usually look to who will be the drivers of tomorrow. Over the past few years, the names Michael Andretti and Al Unser Jr. were always thought of as the " young chargers ", the definite drivers of tomorrow. That was a few years ago. In case you may not have realized it, tomorrow has already unfolded for these young drivers.

Michael Andretti has established himself as one of about ten drivers that are seriously capable of winning an Indy car race. As the eldest son of a racing legend, it was inevitable that Michael would pursue a race driving career. The Andretti name has been a household one for many years. In the 1990's, the Andretti name will certainly remain an active part of the racing fan's vocabulary.

When I thought of drivers to interview for this one-on-one section, I wanted a relatively new driver (Scott Pruett), a seasoned veteran (Rick Mears), and an experienced winning driver. The name Michael Andretti came to mind first. Not only is Mike a great young driver with an even brighter future, I knew that he would be good for a few fiery comments.

Rick Amabile: Can you compare the Lola chassis to the March ?

Michael Andretti: When you go into comparing cars, every race car every year is different. You can compare a '90 Lola to an '89 Lola and they're totally different. It's just like comparing it to a March or whatever. Every car is different in its own way whether it's a Lola or a March. It just depends on the year. The technology and things are changing all the time. So you can't really compare the two.

Amabile: Can you compare the Chevy to the Cosworth ?

Andretti: The Chevrolet is a very smooth running engine with a lot of torque compared with the Cosworth. The Cosworth short stroker....I think at top end, was not too far off the Chevy. The problem with the Cosworth was that you had to rev it and you had to keep it up in high revs. The Chevy's real advantage is down low, in the low rpms. The thing just has a lot of torque and very smooth power. In other words, you don't have any lag at all, the turbo or anything because it's so strong and stout, so it makes it a lot easier to drive, especially on a road course. The Chevy just basically has the Cosworth beat all the way through the range. It has more horsepower all the way through the ranges, more torque down low. At top end the Cosworth is closest to the Chevy, but it still comes up short.

Amabile: How is the Newman / Haas team organized differently as opposed to the Kraco team ? I mean, Kraco has run two cars in the past.

Andretti: I guess at Kraco, it was really two different teams that I was with. The first year it was with Geoff Brabham (1984), the second year it was with Kevin Cogan. Those two years were tough years really. The team was a little bit disorganized, it wasn't really set up for a two car team. I was finally able to convince Maury Kraines at the end of '85 that we had to do some reorganizing by getting different people in there and going to a one car team. When we did that, I think that was the best move we ever made. We hired on Barry Green and Adrian Newey, our engineer, I think that we had a really strong combination in '86. I think that's when Kraco really made their move. All of the sudden we were competitive and winning. It was like that through '88. Then in '89, an idea came along, of my father and me getting together on the same team. At first we said " no way ", but then the more we thought about it, the more we thought it would work because it would not be a typical two car team such as I had worked with in '84 and '85. Because.... let's face it, I was racing against Geoff Brabham and Kevin Cogan; I had to beat those two, because if I didn't, I didn't look too good. There was too much inner team rivalry, among the mechanics and the whole bit. It was just not healthy. Where now, with our team the way it's structured, we all have a common goal. Being father and son we work together all the way through until the race, because of that, I think that the team itself is more unified. When we get on the race track, it's a different story, I mean it's every man for himself. In the end, I think we come up with better race cars because we work together. The other way that it's restructured....in '84 and '85 we were totally mechanic oriented. Mechanics ran the show. In '86, '87, and '88, the engineer was introduced and he started to become stronger, but still (Team Manager) Barry Green still wanted to run the show. So it was still half mechanic, half engineer

In this modern era of racing, sponsors place many more demands on their drivers. Michael signs autographs at this in-store appearance to promote his sponsors products.

oriented. Now in '91, it's totally engineer oriented. Engineers are running the show here. I think that nowadays that's the best combination, because of the way that the series has gone. It's become a much more engineer oriented series, such as Formula One. I think that's the evolution that I had and I think that it's going forward every step of the way.

Amabile: Working with your dad, what have you learned the most while being his team mate ?

Andretti: I don't know if I can really point out one thing. I think we've just have been able to bounce ideas off each other, I think we've been able to learn from each other. But, outright having one thing that I've learned, I can't really say. I think that it's just been a nice experience that we've just been able to work on certain things because two heads are better than one every time. It's also really good because we don't always have the same views on things. There's times we're very different, the way we look at things, so that even makes it better because we broaden our scope of ideas.

Amabile: Is it finally nice to have a teammate that you can trust ?

Andretti: Yeah, right. I mean I felt that I could trust....well maybe not Brabham, but I felt that I could trust Kevin, but still I had to keep some things to myself and he had to keep some things, just because of our careers. But here it's a different deal, because if I don't do well, I hope dad does well.

Amabile: When you were a little boy, or just growing up, did you ever dream of teaming with your dad, or did you even think about that ?

Andretti: I never thought about it at all. When I was little I didn't expect I'd be driving against him! Let alone on the same team. I mean I always felt that I was going to drive, but I didn't think he'd still be driving when I was driving.

Amabile: Okay, here we go, the so called Andretti jinx. Does it ever upset you that the media makes such a big

A Chevy engine was all that Mike needed to resore his winning ability. (Ed Locke photo)

22

thing of it, especially at Indy ?

Andretti: I don't get upset, it's all part of the deal. I wish I could explain why we don't have good luck there, but I can't explain why we have good luck at other places! You know, that's the way the ball bounces. Whatever's meant to be, is meant to be. That's the way you have to look at it and there's nothing you can do about it. All you can do is go out and try 110 percent every time. And if you do, if you keep at it long enough, you're going to win. A jinx is not really a jinx, it's just timing more than anything. You know, I could just as easily won two Indianapolis' as I did two Michigans. It's just the way the timing was, that I was suppose to do well in August instead of May.

Amabile: Do some of your father's frustrations at Indy make you a little more intense at Indy ?

Andretti: No, because actually with his frustrations I've learned a lot, to basically not put all my eggs in one basket. In other words , if I don't win Indy in my career, I don't want to feel that my career's been a failure. It's just another race, and that's all it really is. I think for my career it would probably be the greatest thing that ever happened. But me personally, I'd rather win a championship than just that one race.

Amabile: Really ! The Indy car title ? Really ?

Andretti: Yeah, personally deep down inside, but I think for my career it would do me better by winning Indy. There's two different ways to look at it: career-wise and personal satisfaction. Because, lets face it, winning Indy, it has to be your day and there's a lot of luck involved. So you don't get that same personal satisfaction as you would say through a year of working at it and getting to your goal.

Amabile: What sort of business interests do you have on the side ?

Andretti: We're in all sorts of things. The biggest thing is we (along with his father) have three car washes and a Hanna distributorship. That and we have some other things that we're involved in, local business and stuff.

Amabile: How did your Formula One testing deal with McLaren evolve ?

Andretti: Well, I've been interested in Formula One for quite a while. Tyler Alexander, who works for McLaren and used to work Newman / Haas, basically put in the word to (McLaren boss) Ron Dennis that I was coming over to England to meet with some people and some teams and basically we set up a meeting with Ron. From there, he basically put a proposal on the table for the testing team and the rest is history.

Amabile: What was your first impression of an F-1 car to drive ?

Andretti: Well, it's just a different animal. It's a different car and you just have to adapt to it. It just does different things and you have to do different things to adjust to it. It just has a different feel. I don't want to go into it too much because I'm sure that McLaren's competiters are wondering the same thing.

Amabile: Does it feel lighter than an Indy car to drive?

Andretti: Yeah, it does. It has a lighter feeling to it in the steering, and a little bit of a harsher ride to it.

Amabile: Is it faster in pickup ?

Andretti: Yeah, it definitely has better acceleration because of the weight, it basically has the same horsepower as an Indy car, but it's 400 pounds lighter so it obviously has better acceleration.

Amabile: Does that extra 400 pounds make an Indy car feel like driving a tank ?

Andretti: To be honest, no. There's just a different feel to it.

Amabile: Is F-1 more of an emotional challenge because of your Italian heritage and your father's success, or is it more of a professional challenge ?

Andretti: Nah, to me it's a professional challenge really. The emotional thing, with dad winning and stuff is fine, but it's the same thing in Indy cars, you know he's won everything in Indy cars too. I'm doing it because I want to win, not because dad's done it, it's because I want to do it. So it's more professional to me.

Amabile: I talked to Rick Mears about possibly doing F-1 and he said he was just curious to see if he was as good as some of the F-1 drivers. Are you curious to see if you're as good as some of the F-1 drivers ?

Andretti: I feel very strongly that our top six drivers are as good as their top six drivers. As long as I feel that way, I feel that I can be competitive over there. I think that Eddie Cheever is a perfect example. He came over thinking that he would basically jump in and blow our doors off! I think that he was running with a car that's more competitive than he's ever had in Formula One. He had a Lola and a Chevy, which is basically what we had. I mean, it's the same exact deal, and it was a pretty good team too. He ended up running in the same spot, qualifying in the same spot as he was in Formula One. So I think that Eddie is a good example for us to look at.

Amabile: Do you get along with Cheever ?

Andretti: Yeah, he's all right. I don't have any problems with anybody.

Amabile: Do all of the CART - FISA battles hurt your negotiating with F-1 teams at all ?

Andretti: No, that hasn't come in to play at all.

Amabile: With the FISA Super license that is required to drive in Formula One, you can't do both Indy cars and Formula One.

Andretti: I wouldn't do it anyway. I think that's one thing that I've learned off dad. He burned himself out on trying to do both. I would only do one of them.

Amabile: Would doing F-1 mean moving your family to Europe part-time ?

Andretti: No, I don't think I'd move over there. I think I'd still live over here being where I live on the East coast, close to New York, I'm only an hour drive to the Newark airport. I'm pretty close to Europe, it's only a six hour flight.

Amabile: I don't think that there's ever been a second generation driver in Formula One ?

Andretti : Yeah, I think that Gary Brabham was the first.

Amabile: Yeah, but I mean a competitive one. If you went over there and even just did medium, that would be great.

Andretti: Yeah, I'd love to. I'd love to be competitive.

Amabile: Do you think that the F-1 drivers look down at the Indy car drivers ?

Andretti: I don't think the drivers do. I think that the teams do because they don't know really what we're all about, and they don't want to know. They tend to, you know, put themselves up on a pedestal.

Amabile: Yeah, but you'd think since we've got some big name drivers over here, it would be really good for their marketing effort ?

Andretti: Nah, they don't really look at that. I'm finding that out.

Amabile: What has been the scariest moment that you 've ever had in a race car ?

Andretti: In a race car....Oh yeah, I guess I can probably think of one. In 1990 at Mid-Ohio, I lost my rear brakes, that was a scary one. I went off the track and hit a tire barrier. About another eight feet to the right and I would have went head on into a gaurd rail. I was trying to avoid the tires, but then I could see that there was nothing there, I took all the run off. I didn't even know that there was a guard rail around. When I got out of the car, I looked down and saw the guard rail and thought " Oh my God ". I didn't know that I was that close to hitting anything that was solid.

Amabile: How does that effect you when you get back in to a car ? I mean, that's got to take a lot of balls to get back into a car in such a relatively short race weekend such as Mid-Ohio.

Andretti: I don't know, you just have to block it out at the time. I had to block it out at the time because I knew that I had a job to do by getting back to the pits and get into the spare car and get a couple of laps in it and go out and qualify. I didn't really have any time to think about it, you just do it, and worry about it later. I was lucky to get in the spare car and go out and get on the pole.

Amabile: Hard day at the office ! When something like that happens, do you just look back and say " Whew, what a day " ?

Andretti: A little bit, yeah.

Amabile: When you're driving an Indy car, do you double-clutch ?

Andretti: No, you don't have time. Sometimes I will during the race.

Amabile: Do you brake with your right or left foot ?

Andretti: Right foot. A lot of drivers brake with their left foot. Rahal, Al Unser Jr., Rick Mears, I think they all brake with their left foot. I think that's because those guys were brought up around oval racing. I brake with my left foot on ovals. You use your left foot to brake just to get the car set. Sometimes you're on the brakes and the throttle at the same time, to keep the revs up. I think that most all of the Formula One drivers brake with their right foot.

Amabile: Do you work out with weights or anything to keep in shape ?

Andretti: No.

Amabile: Well at least you 're honest about it ! I know a lot of drivers say that they work out, but they really don't. What do you do to keep in shape ?

Andretti: I like to play golf and tennis.

Amabile: Do you have any special diet ?

Andretti: I don't during the off-season. During the season I try to stick to a high carbohydrate diet.

Amabile: What was it like growing up with the Andretti name when you were little ?

Andretti: I don't know....I mean, I can't really say that I knew any different. I didn't know any different than if, you know, my dad worked in a steel mill or whatever. I was always into racing. I didn't play on any sports teams. All of the people that I used to hang around with were usually older than I was, all my friends were usually older than me. My parents own 640 acres in the Pocono mountains, so we used to go up there on the weekends. I used to ride snowmobiles and other kinds of motorized stuff. I think that's what really caused me to do this (race driving) because there were no limits up there, you know speed limits, so I could just ride and have fun and do whatever I wanted. As far as everything else, all that I can remember was that dad was gone a lot. When he got home, it was more like quality time rather than quantity time, you know , when he was home, we made the most of it. So it was definitely quality time rather than quantity time.

1986 saw Andretti and the Kraco team finally make it into victory circle and lose their "also ran" status forever. (Dennis Torres photo)

One-On-One With Scott Pruett

Breaking into Indy car racing was never meant to be an easy task. Over the past few years, Scott Pruett has graduated from being a two-time IMSA GTO champion, to driving for the affluent TrueSports team. I had a chance to sit down with Scott at Laguna Seca, the final event of the 1990 Indy car season, and discuss several things that have developed over the past couple of seasons.

Rick Amabile : Breaking into Indy car racing when you went to Dick Simon Racing , did you expect to do as much work with sponsors and marketing going into the deal ?

Scott Pruett : I did just because of my backround and how I started racing go-carts. A good person who pointed that out to me was Bruce Jenner, as far as you have to be a good athlete , but you also have to be aware of the marketing aspect of it, marketing yourself, taking care of the sponsors, interviews, etc. I'd say that clear back to '82, '83, I've been very conscious of that aspect of motor sports. I think that's probably one of the reasons why I've gotten to this point in time, you know being aware of those things and understanding them. The bottom line is that we are all involved in a sport that is really a form of entertainment for people. We're just entertainers, we love doing what we're doing, don't get me wrong, but you have to understand that we are entertainers and take the time with the marketing aspect of it and be aware of it.

Amabile: Did you go out and hire a P.R. person to raise money for the Dick Simon ride at Long Beach in 1988 ?

Pruett : No, not at all. I got a little bit of money from some of the people that I was involved with in Trans Am, a lot of it came out of my own pocket as an investment in my future. That's where most all of it came from, I'd say that 90 percent of it came from that. I had saved my money to do something, I thought that maybe with my involvement with Ford, I thought maybe I was going to go overseas to do some Formula One stuff and that didn't work out, so at the time the best thing to do was.... what better way to prove to people your abilities then get out there and show them.

Amabile: That was a big risk though, I mean we're talking about 50 grand to buy a ride for a race weekend.

Pruett: It was a big gamble, it was a real big gamble, But it felt right. And fortunately,..... I've always been a strong believer in doing the things that feel right to you even though you may not understand them.

Amabile: What was it like trying out for the TrueSports ride?

Pruett: It was tough, there was a lot of pressure because that is such an interesting thing to do.... you have to push as hard as you can, but you can't crash the race car. At the end of the day, everybody looks at numbers on how fast you go. Everything else being equal, they look at how fast you go, so there was a lot of pressure. You had to be careful because you'd lose everything if you crashed the car. There was a real fine line there on pushing it, a lot of pressure, nervousness and excitement.

Amabile: What's it like going to work for the mighty Budweiser and being the All-American Budweiser driver ?

Pruett: Budweiser is a great company to work for. I was involved with them once before just doing one race. They do things right or they don't do them at all. Over the years I've been involved with some sponsors who just put dollars into it and didn't understand how to capitalize on it. That's the exciting part about being involved with Budweiser, they understand how to use it, whether it's advertising, T.V. commercials or promotion. They know how to get the most mileage out of their relationship with a team.

Amabile: Do you do a lot of in store appearances and company functions?

Pruett: Everything, all sorts of things. Anywhere from convenience store conventions, to doing stuff with their employees, to doing stuff with distributors, to doing stuff with their wholesalers like at a bar or something and signing autograghs. Whatever they feel that they need me for, they do a lot of different things.

Amabile: So you just jump in and say " use me".

Pruett: Sure, we live and learn , some things are real successful and other things are not. It's a continual learning process as we go along.

Amabile: What do you think when you turn on the ol' T. V. set and see a Budweiser commercial that features you. Do you ever see that and think..."Wow,

Indianapolis can be a tough track to figure out for some drivers, however Scott managed to gain Co Rookie of the Year honors in 1989. (Doug Wendt photo)

I'm driving the Budweiser car," when you probably dreamed about it just a few years ago?

Pruett: Sure, I'm just real honored to be a part of their team. It's exciting.... there's a real romance with racing, especially with Indy cars, and then to be with one of the most successful sponsors in racing, all those things together .... I'm just honored to be a part of it.

Amabile: You were pretty involved with the new car that TrueSports has built. What have you learned about the design process of building a new car?

Pruett: Over the years, I've always been real interested in what was going on with the team, with the cars, with the engines, with everything, every aspect of it. So I enjoy going in there every day and seeing what's going on. You learn where the conception comes from, you learn why they did something one way, instead of doing it the other. You learn, I think, a better understanding of the race car itself from a mechanical standpoint, to relate to the engineers better. Overall, I think you just get a better understanding of that whole race car that you're in.

Amabile: When you were injured at West Palm Beach, Florida, can you describe what the team was doing that day ?

Pruett: We were trying a bunch of things on a street course, a simulated street like Long Beach. I had a rear brake failure, and that's happened to about six teams this year (1990). I virtually went straight off at the end of the straight at about...I figured about 135 to 140 mph and hit a cement barrier.

Amabile: Dead center ?

Pruett: Dead center. There was one set of tires there but they weren't tied together so they were just out of the way.

Amabile: Were you conscious the whole time ?

Pruett: Yeah, I remember everything.

Amabile: What's that like ?

Pruett: You know, it's funny because I wasn't scared,...I was pissed off ! Pissed off beyond belief. It was unbelievable. You know, it gives you a real appreciation for friends and family, it gives you appreciation for your body and taking care of it.

Amabile: Were your legs just totally in pain ?

Pruett: My back was sore because I broke my back, my knees were sore, I crushed my left ankle, my right ankle was pinned in the car. All those things.....it was tough, it was tough for everybody, it was tough for the team, it was tough for myself. We had the whole momentum going, winter testing was going great, I had a pretty good '89 season and we were looking forward to the '90 season. The whole thing was tough to swallow. It was bad enough where it was either going to make you or break you, you're either going to get stronger because of it, or you were going to get out of the sport because of it.

Amabile: When they got you out of the car, and you realized how bad your feet were, did you think..."oh my God." " There goes my career" ?

Pruett: Just, "how long until I was going to be back". That was all that I was concerned about. When they got me out of the car, I didn't know how bad things were broken. We didn't know that my back was broken at the time. Originally, when they got me out of the car, I thought that it was going to be about four months. I wasn't expecting the whole season because I didn't know about the back

Amabile: Do you remember going to the hospital ?

Pruett: No, I was out of it. Dr. Baele rebuilt my legs and Dr. Trammell rebuilt my back. I don't remember much of those few days, just bits and pieces.

Amabile: How did the car (89 Lola) hold up ?

Pruett: Considering the impact, I think it was pretty good. The 1991 car has even more precautions built into it. From any adverse situation, you're going to learn a lot from it: how to make better race cars, how to make safer race cars, how to be safer at a track, how to make conditions better overall for everybody. I think that CART itself has learned a lot that we can share with other teams, so it doesn't happen that way again.

Amabile: What's it like rehabilitating once everything was healed ? Did you have to learn to rewalk ?

Pruett: I didn't have to learn how to rewalk....the biggest thing is that you have no strength in your legs. Just getting up on crutches for the first time, I had expected just to get up on them and roll, and I couldn't go hardly 20 feet. My legs were just so weak. The muscle atrophy was unbelievable, I virtually lost all the muscle in my legs. You cannot appreciate how much work it is until you have to do it, until you're in that situation. It's just day in and day out. When I first started, I could not see the light at the end of the tunnel. It was just so much work.... I couldn't see the end of the road. And then as things went along, about four months into it, is when I finally got to a point were I could

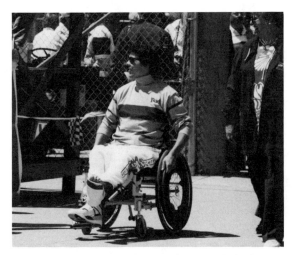

Pruett was forced to observe the 1990 Indy 500 from a wheelchair. Scott has bounced back into full form in 1991. (Louis Rapier photo)

see the light at the end of the tunnel. I saw the point where I could start walking, I could see the point of getting back in a race car, having the strength and flexability back in my legs, having the endurance. It was a tough road.

Amabile: I see where you're into body building now.

Pruett: It was just getting everything back into shape. I really wouldn't call it body building. I use Keiser equipment to keep in shape, and I have a cardio-vascular program.

Amabile: Do you eat a special diet ?

Pruett: No, I just watch what I eat.

Amabile: Do your legs still hurt you ?

Pruett: There's still quite a bit of pain. Not really pain, it's just achiness, everything aches.

Amabile: Is it anything that you could take a couple of Bufferin to cure ?

Pruett: No, it's there forever, you get used to it. There's a lot of pain in my foot because of nerve damage. The doctors say I can't do anything about it, it's just something that you have to get used to. On some days it's worse than others, but you learn how to deal with it.

Amabile: What about when it gets cold ?

Pruett: It's terrible. (laughing)

Amabile: Do you ever go to Rick Mears, or Daly, and get advice ?

Pruett: Sure, they both have been very good throughout the whole thing. Rick told me that he still has a lot of pain in his feet, just because of nerve damage.

Amabile: Just kind of grin and bear it ?

Pruett: Yep, that's all you can do.

Amabile: I see where you' re into broadcasting now. Kind of a second career that happened by accident. Would you like to do that full-time when you retire from racing ?

Pruett: Maybe, that's not really something that I'm looking at. I've enjoyed the opportunity immensely, to work in broadcasting. I have gained a lot of respect for the broadcasters that are out there. The hard work, the hours of studying what they have to do, was something that I didn't appreciate before. I've learned a lot from it

Amabile: A lot of fans look to Little Al or Michael and ask when they're going to go Formula One racing. You said earlier that you possibly wanted to do F- 1, what was the big obstacle there ?

Pruett: The big obstacle there is the stigma of Europeans not understanding.... I don't think it's not understanding, but because they are so separated from us in the United States, they 're not aware of your career, what you do and what's been done, you're not in front of them as much. That's the biggest barrier that you try to break through.

Amabile: But doesn't that piss you off when you win a championship, this is America, they read the American press.

Pruett: Yeah, but they 're not around you. You don't appreciate a driver unless you see him drive. Talk to him and see him, all of those things. Without that it

Scott finished eighth in points in his rookie season, while coming close to victory at Detroit. (ICR photo)

makes it a little bit more difficult, a lot more difficult.

Amabile: When your contract with Truesports is up at the end of '91, and a decent, middle of the road F-1 team approached you, would you do it ?

Pruett: ....Decent, middle of the road, no. It's tough to say because drivers always keep their options open and look at all the opportunities that are out there. It all depends on what my opportunities are here, compared to what my opportunities are there. I want to be in a position to win races. You can't win races if you don't have the equipment that you need to do it. Without being in that position, it's tough to say, yes I would or wouldn't. I would just look at every opportunity that there is available to me.

Amabile: Have you ever talked to any F-1 teams or F-3000 teams ?

Pruett: I've talked to a few F-1 teams, I know a number of the guys. I really haven't thought about that in a long time.

Amabile: When you got back into an Indy car, do you use muscles that you can't work into shape with weights ?

Pruett: No....you just have to learn what muscles you use and then put together a workout program around that. I do a certain amount of things with free weights, that help me work on those muscles that you wouldn't necessarily work on with other equipment. The biggest thing you can do is just get yourself into the best overall shape you can. You need flexability, cadiovascular endurance, muscle endurance and muscle strength. When you 're in a car, and you have muscles that bother you, you focus on those with other types of programs. After racing in 1989, my trainer (Phil .Disabeto) and I worked together on a number of different things to help those areas.

Amabile: How many hours a day did you use to spend rehabilitating ?

Pruett: As much as they would let me. At one point, I spent eight hours a day, five or six days a week.

Amabile: Do you look forward to working out every-day?

Pruett: Sure. It becomes obsessive, it becomes a real obsessive thing. Even before my crash, you feel so much better when you're working out and taking care of yourself. I can't even remember the last time I was sick. I take vitamins and watch what I eat...I think that physical health and mental health go hand-in-hand.

Amabile: What side interests do you have ?

Pruett: I'm interested in a lot of things. As far as hobbies, I've gotten into building some furniture. I really enjoy that. I grew up around metal fabrication and a lot of contemporary furniture these days is metal, glass and marble. For fun I've been doing it more and more.

Amabile: What does your dad (Robert) do ?

Pruett: He's in aerospace. He works for a company named Aerojet, Their real claim to fame was that they built the re-entry engines for the space shuttle.

Amabile: Where do you live now ?

Pruett: I have a place in Lake Tahoe and a place in Dublin, Ohio. I'm going to be building most of my furniture for my place in Tahoe.

Amabile: Whenever you 're at home and you go down to the 7-11 or whatever to get something, do people often recognize you ?

Pruett: Not as much in Tahoe, but in Columbus, sure all the time. It's an exciting feeling. It's getting more and more, it's getting to the point where people recognize me at airports and things like that.

Amabile: Does that ever bother you ?

Pruett: No. Most people are real good where if I'm busy, I'll tell them I'm real busy and I can't spend any time with them, maybe come back later. Generally, sure, I like to spend a couple of minutes with them and say hi. It's flattering to me.

Amabile: Do you ever walk into a store and see one of those Scott Pruett cardboard cut-outs and laugh ?

Pruett: (laughing) Sure, I just kind of chuckle to myself, it makes you feel good. It's almost embarrassing because when you see yourself, you 're almost embarrassed.

Amabile: Good luck in '91.

Pruett: Thanks, I'm really looking forward to doing the full season. Getting back into shape fully, working with the new car, it's something I've been looking forward to for a long time.

At the race track, crews remain totally serious and dedicated to their work, but away from the track, things can be a little different. (Dan Boyd photo)

When I sat down and outlined this book, I wanted to write something that would be extremely fun to read. My 1990 book was sometimes critized for not having any anecdotes. So I thought to myself, yeah, that's right. They want anecdotes, I'll give them some anecdotes that they 'll never forget.

About this time I found myself thinking about the good old days, and then thought to myself, perfect! All I had to do was talk to some of my friends that I have met or worked with over the years and have them recall some of their "Tales From The Road".

Working in the profession of motor racing has all sorts of advantages and disadvantages. Perhaps one of the advantages is getting to see the United States and sometimes the world. As we all know, travel can involve a lot of fatigue. Sometimes it's fun to rid oneself of this fatigue by letting off some steam. Since most of the people that are involved in racing are relatively young, letting off steam can lead to instances that will be remembered for a lifetime.

Working in and around Indy car racing for the past ten years or so, I have participated in and witnessed quite a few of these instances. Sometimes, I think back to the "good old days" and find myself laughing about certain situations and pranks that I have seen, participated in, or at least heard about.

When I was younger, I was once needling an older person about something to the point of excess. The older person turned to a colleague and stated, " The exuberance of youth knows no better ". From that point on, I have really liked the word exuberance. Needless

to say, I've met a lot of exuberant people in racing. I have had the pleasure to actually work with some of these high-spirited, full-of-life, uninhibited people.

When I first approached the following people about participating in the section, their first reaction was okay, then laughter, then ooohh...many of their minds went to the editing stage. What followed were questions such as: " Things that I can tell in a book?" Do I have to use my real name?" "Sure,...where do I start?" " It can't be a pornographic one, right ?" and " I'll have to think of one that won't incriminate me". Some of these stories involve instances that were intentional, while some happened by chance.

The following people are crew members, both active and inactive, or other people that work in Indy car racing. I hope you enjoy this as much as I enjoyed gathering the following stories.

Wayne Eaton,
Bayside Racing

Probably the most outstanding one that won't get me in too much trouble, was probably at Indy in '88. After the race awards banquet, we went back to the place where we were staying (hotel name withheld). We continued to party until about three of four in the morning. I decided to light some fireworks in the hall way, rockets and smoke bombs and some other things. There were some girls there that were taking pictures of me standing there next to Roman candles, shooting them down the hallway. That was probably my luckiest one that I got away with, without being caught. I burned a hole in the carpet. It woke everybody up, the whole hall was full of smoke, but I didn't get caught. Somewhere some girl has a picture of me with a lighter in my hand, with the fireworks going off down by my feet. It was our last day of staying in Indy, so that was kind of the tension breaker. Thrash the hotel room and get out of there !

In 1987 at Indy, we discovered that our electric pit cart was missing. The Safety Patrol notified us that a cart had been spotted up in the turn four infield. So I went down there and saw these guys jumping up and down on the back of it, all of them drunk. I walked right up to them and one guy jumped off the back of it, throwing a fist at me. I threw a fist back and he went down. Then his friends threw their beer bottles down at the cart. I finally got everybody off of it, and everyone started applauding for me, even this guy's friends! There was a lot of people around. There must have been about five or six thousand people all in that corner watching this happen. I drove the cart about a hundred feet and it had a flat tire and had run out of juice. I had to have it towed back to Gasoline Alley.

We (the Kraco team) were on an airplane one time and Phil LePan was sitting about three rows behind me. The stewardess came by and I said "hey, you see that guy back there, he's got a bomb ! " So about halfway through the flight, the Captain comes back and takes me to the back of the plane and says, " I could have you put up on Federal charges" and so on. I got out of that one too! I was definitely lucky on that one. They never said anything to Phil.
The stewardess knew that I was only kidding, but she wanted to make a point to the Captain. It was quite embarrasing after a while because (team manager) Barry Green was sitting right in front of me.

Kent Gerhardt, Former Lead Mechanic, Kraco Racing

We're in the (Kraco team's) Suburban, going out to test at Willow Springs. It was our first test with Bobby Rahal in late 1988. Me, Trev (Westin), Tony (Van Dongen) and Phil (LePan) were driving along and Trev gets this idea that he wants to get a picture of the Space Shuttle. So we drive up to the front gate at Edwards Air Force Base (near Willow Springs) and we see two lanes with this deceiving sign that said something like left lane stop, the right lane had an arrow like go right through. So I slow down and pull to the right and go right through. Now all of the sudden, we're on the base. We get about three miles into the base

and we're looking around for a gift shop to buy a picture or poster of the Space Shuttle. So we're driving through there and all of the sudden, here comes one of those MP cars, coming the other way on the road. As soon as he passed us, he looked in his rear view mirror and turned on his lights and turned around. I noticed this and I told Trev, "oh shit, he's after somebody". Well I'll be damned if he didn't pull us over ! The guard got out of his car and came up to the Suburban with his hand on his gun ! So he asks us what we're doing there. Tony said "we're looking for a doughnut shop". I told him, "no, we're looking for a souvenir shop". So he starts interrogating us ! He made everybody get out but me. It's cold and windy and he made them stand in front of the truck. So he checked my license, of course I've got one guy from Australia, one guy from Canada and one guy from England riding with me, so I was looking real good ! The guard thought that we were crashing the gate, trying to get secrets! So he checks my license and this and that, then they escorted us back to the gate. They had one MP car in front of us and one in back. Here's this Suburban, this urban assault vehicle, with police escorts driving back to the main gate! The guard then ticketed me for not stopping at the gate. As it turned out, there was this lady guard in the booth when we first passed by, but she was all haunched over talking on the phone. We laughed all the way back to Willow Springs ! We were laughing our asses off! When I went inside the guard shack, when they were giving me the ticket, I looked outside at the Suburban and the thing was shaking because those guys were laughing so hard ! I don't think the Space Shuttle was even in town. We made a good impression on Rahal for the first test by telling him this story, he just laughed too.

We used to have a contest to see which one of us could slam the rental car door the hardest when we got out of the car. We were testing at Laguna Seca and we had this Ford Taurus. We went out to eat one night and we got out of the car and....I won the contest, the window broke! Of course it was raining that night, so Ihad to cover it up with plastic. The worst part was telling Barry (Green) about it the next day. He really didn't get mad about it. We returned the car to the rental car company and they never said a word ! It didn't cost me anything.

In 1989 we were in Michigan for the 500, I was in a rental car with Phil (LaPan), Trev (Westin) and Wayne (Eaton). Phil was driving, Trev was in the front passenger seat. So here comes Tony (Van Dongen) driving this big Cadillac that was also rented. Tony comes up and started tailgating us on a freeway off-ramp. Trev sees this and reached his foot over and slammed on the brake ! All of the sudden, we see Tony's eyes get as big as quarters. He hits us, Phil keeps driving and as the cars separate, Tony's front grill came out, rolled underneath the car and he ran over it ! So he pulled over to the side of the road to pick it up. So we laugh all the way to the track. Tony drives up to the track with this big black hole where there used to be a grill. In the mean time, someone who knew who we were stopped and asked Tony if he should go and tell Barry (Green) that he had been involved in an accident ? Tony said "no, no, no don't say anything"! So we got some tie-wraps and tied the grill back on and took it back to the rental car company. They never said a word !

Kyle Moyer
Galles / Kraco Racing

We (the Galles team) were at Michigan in 1988. I was in the hotel sleeping and I was rooming by myself. All of the sudden, I hear a bunch of the guys from the team outside talking and laughing and goofing around. It was still dark outside, but I knew that we had to get up early that morning for the race. So I got up, took a shower and shaved, and got all ready to go to work. So I go outside to get ready to go to the track, then I discovered that a few of the guys that I heard earlier were just getting back from the bar ! It was 3:30 in the morning !

In '85, we were in Portland. So a couple of us get off work at the track, and we were headed down to see the Super Modified races. We were headed down the highway in this van, and I was in the back with Roy shooting off these M-100 firecrackers. So we're shooting them out the back window of the van. We were watching the firecrackers go off underneath all these cars. So we threw one out and didn't see anything blow up, so we figured that that one must have rolled off the side of the highway. So we get ready to light off another one, and all of the sudden, boom! When we threw it out, it landed in the spare tire that was mounted outside the van! It shattered the back window and dented in the back door, but we were alright.

We (the Galles/Kraco team) were at Laguna Seca at the last race of 1990. We're in the hotel sleeping at about 3:00 in the morning. All of the sudden, the fire alarms go off. So everybody bails out of the hotel. The reason the fire alarms went off was because one of our mechanics was down in the garage beneath the hotel burning the tires off on the rent-a-car. All of the tire smoke set off the fire alarms and cleared the entire hotel !

We (the Dan Gurney Racing team) were having a pig roast at Lance Gibbs' place in Indy, in 1984. It was about the time when everyone was making those little oxygen / acetylene bombs. So Chalkie and Andy (Riggs) were in Gurney's transporter and they got this idea that they were going to make the world's biggest oxy / acetylene bomb. So they get a 30 gallon trash bag and start filling it up with the perfect blend of oxygen and acetylene. So they get it all full and start to tie it up. About this time Lance Laughlin walks in the transporter and says, " Hey guys, have you ever heard of static electricity setting those things off ?" About that time we all hear this boooom! It blew Chalkie to the back of the truck, blew Andy through the dressing room lockers and blew Lance out the door ! There were no broken bones, but Chalkie couldn't hear for about two months. The explosion blew Andy's shirt off and singed all the hairs on his chest. We all died laughing! So at this point we were all paranoid that Dan (Gurney) would find out about it and nail us on it. I mean, there were plastic bags everywhere and we dented parts of the truck. So everyone was trying to keep Dan from finding out. So about a week later he comes up and throws three packs of trash bags down on the work bench and says " I think these are static proof boys, if you want to use these !"

Tony Van Dongen
Ganassi Racing

We were on a Formula One charter flight, going to Watkins Glen for the American Grand Prix in 1977. The flight departed from London. It was a flight made up of several teams, drivers, mechanics, owners, everyone involved. I was working on the Surtees team at the time. The plane was a Canadian Pacific DC-8. Of course it was all Formula One people, so that's the biggest mistake they could make to begin with. We're half way over the Atlantic and this huge pillow fight started among the crews in the back. The drivers and owners were up front in first class. So there's pillows flying everywhere when someone decided to rip open one of the pillows, so everyone started ripping open pillows. There were feathers flying everywhere. I was sitting behind Mo Nunn and Clay Regazzoni who were playing backgammon at the time. All of the sudden this pillow comes over and just knocks the board flying, so they storm up to the front of the plane. We covered the stewardesses in racing decals from head to toe. The thing that really did us in was somebody, I won't tell his name because he's actually a current chief Formula One designer, threw a stink bomb up near the flight deck. Needless to say, the pilot didn't like that at all. Then, all of the sudden, Bernie Ecclestone (who is now the VP of Formula One) comes to the back of the plane and stood there. Of course everyone got quiet, like a bunch of school kids. So Bernie announces " If anyone throws another pillow, they will never work in Formula One again". As soon as he turned his back to go back up front, this pillow goes flying over his head ! Everyone denied it so he didn't do anything. As soon as we got to Syracuse, NY and the cleaning crews came aboard, took one look and walked off ! We actually met the flight crew that were on that plane some months later when we were going to the Dutch Grand Prix, and they said that plane had to be put out of action for two weeks. As it turned out, all of the feathers blocked up all of the air conditioning and ventilation ducts. I think because of that flight, they wouldn't take all of the teams on one plane anymore. There's been plenty of rental cars wrecked, but we took out an entire DC-8.

We (team Lotus) were at the Swedish Grand Prix in 1978. I was doing the pit board for Ronnie Peterson who was Swiss. So I'm out doing the pit board during the race, and all of the sudden this man appears on the pit wall right by where I was working in a really nice suit and dark glasses with this lady. So I turn to them and told them to basically get lost. The man said " do you know who you 're talking to" ? I said" no". As it turned out, they were the Swedish Royal Family !

Paul "Ziggy" Harcus
Galles / Kraco Racing

About ten years ago, our team went to a race and the hotel reservations got messed up so they put three guys in one room. So the third guy had to sleep on a roll-away. The guys were down at the bar one night and the guy that was sleeping on the roll away went up and went to sleep. So the other guys who he was rooming with went up to go to bed and saw the guy on the roll-away who was basically passed out after drinking too much. So they partially folded up the bed with him in it, and rolled it into the hallway. Then the guys discovered that the elevator door was big enough to fit the roll-away through. It was a really nice hotel with big elevators. So they pushed the bed into the elevator with him still sleeping in his underwear and was half out of the sheets. So the guys pressed the lobby button and went back to their room. So the guy wakes up to the security guards who were tapping him on the shoulder and asking him "what's going on" ?

When I was working in Formula One, I took some time off to visit some friends of mine in Norway. So on the last night of my stay they threw a party for me. These friends of mine worked at the hospital as anesthesiologists. I didn't remember too much of the party, but when I woke up the next morning I had a hell of a hangover. These two guys were sitting on my bed saying "how do you feel". So I said that I felt okay, I've got a hangover, but I'm okay. Then they say "how's your leg" ? I said "what do you mean" ? So I get up to get out of bed and the next thing I look down and my leg's in plaster up to my knee. So they started telling me what had happened the night before. They told me that we were fooling around and that I fell off of the second story balcony and broke my leg. So I'm thinking "how am I going to get back to England and go back to work"? So then they started telling me that when they brought me back from the hospital the night before that "I was complaining that my urine was purple". So I tell them "no way, get out of here". So I went to the bathroom and sure enough my urine was bright purple! So I came running out of the bathroom and told them and they said "oh no, you 've got internal bleeding". So they sent me to this doctor who lived downstairs. He tells me "Yeah, you 've got internal bleeding, we're going to have to take you back to the hospital". About that time I was almost in tears. So finally they just started laughing! What had actually happened was that night they gave my some crystals that they use to test peoples kidneys. If your kidneys are good, it actually comes through purple. What they did was they put these crystals on a sandwich for me. I had one bite of the sandwich and decided I didn't want the sandwich, so I gave it to the dog ! So all around the backyard there were all of these purple spots! They managed to put some in my beer, before I fell asleep. I didn't fall off the balcony at all, they just put my leg in plaster for a joke.

Bill Vukovich Jr.

This was back when I was working for Simpson Race Products. I was getting ready to go to the Meadowlands and take care of our Indy car guys. It's eight in the morning on a Wednesday and I had to be at the Meadowlands at eight the next morning, and I'm in Indianapolis. So about that time, I get a call from Mr. Simpson. "Vuky, Vuky, there's a stock car race at Pocono this weekend, you got to get there today and service those guys then go on to the Meadowlands". So I jump in my van without looking at my calender and I drive to Pocono. I finally get there at about seven that night so I got a hotel for the night figuring that I would get up bright and early and go out to the track. So I show up at the race track the next morning and sure enough there's a little activity going on. So I drive inside and I see Corvettes and what appeared to be a little SCCA deal going on. So I'm trying to be cool and kind of walking around and looking things over. So I asked this guy "when do the stock car guys get here?" The guy says "I don't know, this is a SCCA deal, I don't know anything about a stock car race" So I think that this guy's in the twilight zone because he doesn't know that there's a stock car race going on here this weekend. So I'm wondering where all of these NASCAR guys are at ? So I drive out of the track and I go to the front office to see the Mattiolli's, who own the track. So I ask them when will the stock car guys get here ? So they asked me if I had come to Pocono for the Stock car race ? I said yeah, and I explained my whole situation. So they said "yeah, there's a NASCAR race but you 're about a week and a half too early !"

Here's an oldie but goodie, *R.A.*

Me and Gary Bettenhuasen were at the Pocono 500 back in the early '70s. Gary towed his midget over there with him, because there was suppose to be a midget race nearby. So we got through the Indy car practice late one afternoon, so Gary wanted to go to Flemington and race his midget. So we got everything loaded up and he throws me this road map and says "find Flemington". So I looked up Flemington in the map and we drove to Flemington. It was about a two hour trip. So we roll into Flemington about 5:30pm and we stop at this little hamburger joint. So we ask this guy "where's the race track". The guy says, "we don't have a race track in this town". So I tell Gary, "this guy doesn't know what the hell he's talking about, lets just finish our hamburgers and we 'll go down to a service station and ask directions to Flemington raceway". So we come to find out that there was no race track in this this town, zero, zilch. So we get on the phone and we found out what had happened. Gary told me to find Flemington, so I found Flemington, Pennsylvania. We were in the right town, but we were in the wrong state! The race track we wanted was in Flemington, New Jersey. We were about 150 miles west of Flemington, New Jersey. The only good thing about it was that we went back to Pocono and I beat Gary out of 60 bucks playing pool.

Trev Westin
Newman / Haas Racing

We (the Kraco team) were at the Indy car in Milwaukee and were driving down to Chicago to watch a baseball game while we had some time off. There was about six of us in this Lincoln Town car. We had this guy on the team named Dennis who used to go to the University of California at Santa Barbara. Dennis was always wearing this baseball hat from UCSB. So we're driving along the freeway and Tony (Van Dongen) tossed the hat out of the window. So of course Dennis was real upset about it. So to make up for it, we bought him this hat that looked like a big slice of Swiss cheese at the baseball game. So the next day we were driving to the race track on the same freeway and all of the sudden we spot Dennis' hat laying on the side of the freeway. Dennis was all relieved that he was going to get his hat back. I was driving, so I came up to the hat and jammed on the brakes. So then Dennis jumps out to get his hat. What we found out was that when pulled over and hit the brakes, I stopped directly on top of the hat and shredded it to pieces !

We used to have this electronics engineer at Kraco named Tim, who was the real snobby type. He had this racing bicycle that he took up to Toronto to ride back and forth from the hotel and the track. So the guys put salt in his water bottle, put mustard inside his bicycle helmet and disconnected his brakes. So later we see him go flying out onto the street in Toronto with no brakes and this mustard ring around his head!

Danny Drinan, Former Lead Mechanic,
Kraco Racing

We (the Kraco team) were testing at Phoenix in 1987. As soon as the test was over and everybody was gone, we jumped in our rental cars and headed for the airport. We had rented two Lincoln Town Cars which I was driving one of them. So we decide to take some quick laps around the race track before we leave. So I got the jump on the other car and smoked 'em through turn one and two. At the the end of turn two the pit wall ends on the outside and leads to the road out of the track. So I thought that I would just grab the parking brake and do a U-turn and the end of turn two and drive out the gate. I was going about 60 or 70 mph. So I pull the parking brake and pitched the rear end out, it dismounted both of the rear tires from the wheels and ground down the aluminum rims. So I skid to a stop and we all jump out take the spare tires out of both cars and did a quick pit stop. We got to the airport on time though.

We (the Kraco team) were staying at this hotel (near Mid-Ohio), and I was rooming with Jim Wilson. I was down in the bar and decided to go up and go to bed. By this time big Jim was already asleep. So I come in and I guess I didn't lock the door properly. So I get undressed and go to bed. I was just about ready to fall asleep when I heard the door open. The lights were off and I heard someone rustling around, and in the darkness I saw somebody really big. So I just thought it was Jim. So I hear this guy getting undressed, so I couln't figure out what the hell the deal was. So all of the sudden this guy starts going toward Jim's bed and he says " I'm gonna get you tonight Baaayby" ! So Jim wakes up and says " what's going on ?" Then the guy realized that he was in the wrong room and gathered his clothes and ran out the door !

Rick Amabile

In the early 1980s, I got my first job in Indy car racing working for a team at Indianapolis. I was still in high school at the time and I was able to take three weeks off and go back to Indy. About my third day on the job, one of the mechanics told me to go out to the team's transporter to get something. When I got back to the garage I discovered that all of the doors were closed. A couple of our mechanic's girlfriends were sitting outside so I asked "what's going on" ? " There's a meeting for crew members only ", they declared. So I proudly walked in the garage where this supposed 'meeting' was taking place. As I closed the door behind me I notice that there were these three people asking everybody questions. As soon as one of them saw me he asked our chief mechanic if I was okay ? " He's okay", our chief mechanic replied. The three people turned out to be F.B.I. agents who were investigating a case. They were interviewing everybody on the team. I was one of the last to be interviewed. This woman agent shows me her badge and asked if I would answer some questions? It was just like Dragnet! As she finished the interview, she told me " If you find out the whereabouts of the person in question, please contact your local F.B.I. office." "Okay, sure," I said, "but I live in Fresno, I'm not sure if they even have one there ?"

Ron Dawes, Chief Mechanic, Hemelgarn Racing

We (the Hemelgarn team)were up in Canada, the day after the Toronto race in '88. We were in our rent-a- cars driving to the airport. I was driving one car and Darrell Soppe was driving the other. We were just leaving the hotel parking lot and I was behind Darrell. As we were waiting for the traffic light, I pull up and touch my front bumper with his rear bumper and do a power brake. It took out about a half inch of pavement. By this time the, the whole intersection was filled with smoke, you couldn't see any thing. I stopped doing the peel and as the smoke cleared, I see this cop standing right next to me ! He walks up to the side window and

says "What are you trying to do?". He thought that I was trying to push the other car out into the intersection. As it turned out, this cop was in a really bad mood because he was just getting ready to end his shift and go on vacation. So he has me pull over and called for a police car to come out and have my name pulled up on the computer. As this was happening, I remembered that a few years ago, I had gotten a ticket at Sanair (Canada) and I figured that I'd never be in Canada again so I never payed the ticket. So they look up my name and found that I had a bench warrant for my arrest ! So here we go, 'clink'. So they take me down to the station and arranged for me to go to court the next day. By this time, the cop that arrested me was getting harrassed so bad by the other cops because they knew that we were just screwing around and knew that we worked in racing. He got harrassed so bad by the other cops that it put him in an even worse mood. So I go to court the next day and the judge says " I just want to show that we are friendly to our visitors in our country, that will be $300, take off."

We (the Patrick team) were in Phoenix to do some testing. We had a day off before the test so myself, Owen Snyder and Pete Gibbons were at a shopping mall and decided that we 'd all have our ears pierced as a practical joke. So we go to the race track the next day, Pat Patrick's there along with everybody else. We walk up and we've all got our earings in, and Gordy (Gordon Johncock) freaked out ! He coulnd't believe it. Patrick just laughed.

We were running Pocono in 1988 and Gordy was driving for us. Pocono was always so bad for crashes that the race seemed like the day was run half under the yellow flag. Gordy was always funny on the radio. Under one yellow, he was driving through turn three and spotted this girl in a bikini standing on top of a motorhome. So he calls us up on the radio and says "boy, you should see this one up on this motorhome out here, she's good looking" The next lap, still under yellow, Al Sr. was behind Gordy, so Gordy slows down, gets Al Sr. next to him and starts pointing towards the motorhome. After a while, still under yellow, he starts losing track of what's happening out on the track. The next year, we go back to Pocono, and this girl comes down to the pits and introduces herself to Gordy. As it turned out, it was the girl that was on top of that motorhome the previous year !

Playing For Keeps - A Look Inside Indy Car Safety

Over the last decade, Indy car safety has almost embarrassed that of other forms of motor racing, especially in Formula One. One of the most important aspects is the people who comprise the Indy car safety unit. The approach to safety has been carefully thought out, to not only serve drivers and crews better, but to try to erase the negative danger image of the sport. The general public may still believe that Indy car racing is for daredevils, but inside the sport drivers know full well that the sport's risk element is the lowest that it has ever been.

Certainly motor racing will never be totally safe; it was never meant to be. As followers of the sport, many times we have seen brutal accidents where it seemed that we were witnessing a driver's death, only to see the driver rise from the twisted wreckage and walk away. It's almost like these drivers have nine lives.

Look back to the decades of the 1950's and 60's and count how many of our heroes never made it through that period. The drivers that did make it through that era and are still driving today say that they haven't retired because they feel that they can still be competitive. Underneath all of this second youth must loom the assurance that drivers just don't perish as often as they used to. The question is, would we still see drivers competing in their late forties and fifties if the sport's safety level was as dangerous as it was in the 1950's and 60's ? Some say that they still would, but deep down it's obvious that they are not telling the exact truth. It's pretty obvious that the legends of Indy car

When the cars roll away, the drivers know that they will be in good hands if the worst should happen.
(IMS - Steve Snoddy photo)

racing such as, A.J. Foyt, Mario Andretti and Al Unser Sr., are quite well off financially.

One must wonder why these men who have so much to lose, still compete in what can be the cruelest sport of them all. The answer is certainly Indy car racing's better overall safety conditions.

Over the years, I have noticed, read and even wrote articles that were about safety. Most dealt with response times to the accident scene and boasted of how many firefighters and safety personnel were stationed at an Indy car race. Most of these articles were simply written off of a press release. Press releases are somewhat informative, however they also can be somewhat boring.

To reveal a different angle on the safety aspect of the sport, I decided to go to the soldiers on the front lines, so to speak, or as we know them, the paramedics, doctors and safety workers that arrive on the scene first hand. These people often witness up close the ugliest side of a sport where a participant's mistake can make him pay the ultimate price. Indy car drivers are definitely playing for keeps.

Lon Bromley is the safety director for Championship Auto Racing Teams. The CART safety team was formally known as the Horton safety team. Horton withdrew its involvement due to financial restraints. CART took over the safety team at the Milwaukee event in 1990. Lon is responsible for the 17 medical and rescue personnel on the team. In normal life, Lon

35

is the director of ambulance services at Carbon County Memorial Hospital in Rawlings, Wyoming, which covers about 10,000 square miles. Lon has been with CART for five years, and is in his second year as director of safety.

Rick Amabile: In the mid 1980's when Horton came on, was this whole idea created to try to get rid of the stereotype of racing being so dangerous ? Did they sort of beef up the safety procedures to kind of get rid of that image ?

Lon Bromley: I don't think I'd call it a beefing up. I believe that they saw the need finally to advance not only in speed and high tech in the race car, but also in the safety angle in other areas. One shouldn't move ahead without the other. I think that they finally became more aware that safety was a very important part of racing to be able to provide good care rather than provide just "ho hum" type of stuff on the race track. Even in EMS (emergency medical services) today, the world of EMS is a fairly young and expanding area yet today. There's only been about 10 to15 years of really good quality care in the streets, I think. I'm talking about the paramedics in the street. Before it was always run by morticians and that sort of thing for years and years, most people don't even know that. Volunteer people that would run one person in an ambulance and that sort of thing. Then about 15 years ago suddenly there became an awareness and they began to expand and grow. I think that racing did the same thing, suddenly their eyes were open to the fact that they needed to provide a high standard of emergency care to the racing drivers.

Amabile: When you first arrive at an accident scene, and you know that a drivers been hurt, what's the first thing that you do ?

Bromley: The first thing that we do is immediately make sure that we have an airway, to make sure that the driver is able to breathe properly until we can get him out of the vehicle. We found that when they hit the wall at such high rates of speeds that they "ring their bell" most of the time. Because of that they render themselves unconscious at times. So keeping a good airway, while we get their helmet off,or while we prepare to extricate, or provide some sort of care, is our primary task.

Amabile: Does that knock the wind out of a driver when he hits the wall pretty hard ?

Bromley: It really does. I don't think anyone can really conceive how hard they really come into a wall when you're going 200 miles per hour. It's just an unbelievable impact. Of course it depends on the angle of the car hitting the wall on what may or may not cause injury to the driver.

Amabile: When a driver's unconscious, do you let him just naturally wake up on his own ?

Bromley: Yeah, we always give our driver a few minutes. With the proper head manipulation, we can maintain a good airway, that way we can wait to give the driver the opportunity to come around on his own. The big difference here is that when you're a paramedic in the street, and you get a call for an emergency, you're looking at anywhere from 5 to 15 to20 minutes before you arrive at the scene. So when that emergency team finally arrives at that particular scene, you see a different patient in 20 minutes. At a race track where you witness or arrive on the scene within 5 to 10 seconds, you have an entirely different set of situations. I think that this is something that all our medics have to become aware of. It's such a different setting treating a patient right after impact compared to 10 or 15 minutes down the road in a normal response where the doctor may see them in a half hour upon delivery with an ambulance. This is why we carry a physician with us, they're fully aware of everything that goes on with that driver from the moment of impact, all the way until they're discharged at the end of their stay at the hospital. Our team effort is very unique, you don't find very many doctors and paramedics that work good together. Normally in a street situation, each one works on their own and has their own specialty. Here we work very closely as a team. Our physicians do a lot of things that the paramedics do, the medics sometimes do some of the stuff that the physicians could also do.

Amabile: I've noticed that when you guys extricate drivers that you tend to cut away the side of the tub to get the driver out.

Bromley: We don't cut anything unless it's absolutely necessary to get the driver out. Normally when a car hits a wall, like on an oval track, the right front wheel springs back and hits the cockpit about a quarter of the way down from the top which drives it into the driver. It can drive to the top of the cockpit, into the steering wheel and not allow us to get the wheel out, or it comes down across the lower section of the driver's leg right around the gearshift area. The gearshift linkage bar tends to bend and fold over onto the femur or onto the

At first glance, the mobile CART medical center could resemble a tour bus, until you take a look inside.

leg area. You can't just lift the driver up out of the car because the carbon fiber and such has got the leg entrapped. So we have to cut that away, but we try to cut as little as possible to get the driver out the best way.

Amabile: Do you still use the "jaws of life" that much since the carbon fiber age began ?

Bromley: We still use them. Everybody thinks that the "jaws of life" is just a big spreader. But we also use their small rams, we use their cutters. We've picked up some new equipment for 1991. It depends on the incident, and what we are looking at using. In A. J. Foyt's situation (at Elkhart Lake in 1990) we did because of how he went into the dirt embankment. The clutch and the springs all folded down on to his legs, so in that situation we did use the tool quite a bit.

Amabile: In a severe accident like Foyt's where he was conscious the whole time do you try to just get him out of the car and not worry about the feet so much ?

Bromley: No, we don't operate that way. We want to work as quickly as we can, but the safety to the driver at that point is very important. If you take a driver out who's severely injured too quickly and improperly, you can cause further injury to the driver. We take a few extra seconds to make sure that the stability of the patient is taken care of, cut what we need to cut in order for the driver to be taken out smoothly without causing any additional injuries.

Amabile: In Foyt's case, did you have to cut most of the front end of the car away ?

Bromley: Yeah, we had to cut most of the entire front end of the car and most of the major supports over the mid portion of the car, because of the fact that A. J.'s kind of big so it's kind of tough to get him out to begin with.

Amabile: How did you finally get him out of the car ?

Bromley: Basically we went down the center of the car, split the main supports and spread the springs. His feet were such that it took us a while to make sure where the ankle, how the legs were really injured. Then we spread the car open, just like taking a chicken and cutting down the breast in the center of the chicken and we just laid that open, cut the main supports which cross the cockpit. But the problem is that you can't cut a lot of times, because every time you cut with a certain tool, it presses pieces of the car back down or slashes it into a different direction, which causes it to go into the driver. So that's what's usually the most time consuming, making sure that when you make a cut or spread, it's not causing more of a problem.

Amabile: Do you ever go to the car builders and say "hey, it would be nice if you designed this bulkhead, or whatever, differently" ?

Bromley: Dr. Trammell and Dr. Olvey are very much in to that aspect. They're aware of what the new chassis are like. They speak to the builders, that end is handled mostly by the two physicians.

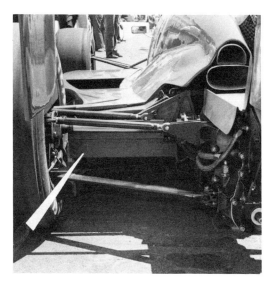

The dreaded tunnel diffusers were suppose to slow cars down in 1990. This left drivers of 1989 cars or older walking a tightrope through the turns at Indianapolis. (Doug Wendt photo)

Amabile: Once you get the driver out of the car, like in the Foyt situation, How do you ready him for the hospital ?

Bromley: Once we get the driver up, he's supported with a special device that we use for a cervical spine. Then he's strapped on to a backboard. In the Foyt situation, all of his injuries were splinted at that point in time. So before he was even moved to the helicopter, he had been administered medication, he had an I.V., he had two splints on his legs, he was packaged and ready to go. The chopper came down, the nurse was given a full report, and the other medic aboard the helicopter was to ride out with the patient.

Amabile: When they bring someone back to the hospital, like in Foyt's situation, there had to be a lot of dirt in the wounds. How do they take it from there ?

Bromley: It's just washed out with water and small brushes. It's a normal procedure, very easy for the O. R. techs at the hospital to do that.

Amabile: Who does the entire CART safety team consist of ?

Bromley: Our entire team is about 20 individuals. That includes EMT paramedics, fire rescue personnel and we've got five doctors. One of my personnel is what I call a track specialist. He's an emergency medical technician also. He has a great knack for being able to put a race track back together after a crash. Whether it is fixing walls, making sure oil spills are taken care of quickly, just getting us back into a green situation real quick.

Amabile: Are you considered a regular paramedic ?

Bromley: I'm considered an EMT -2 or an advanced in the state that I work in. Each state has a different listing and title for their personnel, but they 're all basically EMT paramedics.

The Indianapolis Motor Speedway is undoubtedly the finest motor racing complex in the world. The Speedway has the advantage of fixed safety stations located around the track. During the month of May, the speedway's safety workers, paramedics and doctors provide perhaps the best medical care at any race course in the world. On race day, the Speedway attracts more people in its 320 acres than the entire population of the state of Alaska and the city of Gary, Indiana combined. Aside from the actual racing, when that many people get together in one area, there's bound to be a need for medical services.

Of the estimated 450,000 people that pack the Speedway on race day, about one quarter of one percent, or about 1000 people will need some sort of medical care. Most fans that are seen by medical personnel will only need the so called " Band-aid and aspirin" treatment. The Speedway is equipped with a medical staff of around 250 on race day. The pinnacle of the safety unit in the Hanna Emergency Medical Center, or as most people know it, "the infield hospital". Ironically, the HEMC is not a hospital and is not intended to serve as one. The HEMC is considered to be sort of a large first aid station, or a stopping off point to stabilize a patient who may be seriously injured before the three minute helicopter ride to Methodist Hospital in downtown Indianapolis.

During practice and race day, the Speedway has three paramedics on call on the actual racetrack. Upon seeing and hearing the wicked sights and sounds of a car slamming into a ten inch thick concrete wall at over 200 miles per hour, the safety crews arrive on the scene and experience the dark side of Indy car racing. Motor racing has always been a game of chance. We all know that there will be accidents at a racing event. What we don't know is which driver or drivers will be involved next. In this game of chance, it's sometimes fate that brings a driver into this compromising situation. When the safety crew arrives on the scene, they tend to the unlucky driver who has just picked the shortest straw. John Miller is a paramedic who is in his tenth year with the Indianapolis Motor Speedway.

Rick Amabile: The Speedway safety crew is similar to the CART safety team. After an accident, when you stop the truck and approach the scene, what procedures do you use ?
John Miller: We go in with the concurrance, with the fire department. So we know that they're assessing the scene for any kind of methanol or oil fire. We feel that it's fairly safe unless they deem it not possible to get into the scene, so we feel it's safe for us to go in with them behind us. As we approach the driver we first want to see if they're conscious or unconscious. Because of the crash, no matter how bad it is, we always suspect a neck injury through the mechanism of the accident. So we want to stabilize their neck while we are determining their level of consciousness and determining if their airway is clear or not. The first priority is making sure that we have a clear airway, at the same time we stabilize the spine.
Amabile: Don't you have to kind of work on the neck and the airway at the same time ?

The financial rewards of driving Indy cars seem certainly justified when an accident takes place. Here Johnny Rutherford makes initial contact, resulting in a concussion, at Indy in 1990.
(Ron Weaver photo)

Miller: Yeah, so we have one person maintain a neutral mobilization of the driver's head while the paramedics are working on the airway.

Amabile: What if the driver is completely unconscious ?

Miller: The first priority is to get the level of unconsciousness. What we usually do first is to insert an airway into the driver himself. We insert a tube that goes through the nasal passage and opens to the back of the throat. That gives the driver a clear airway in case there's anything in his mouth. Sometimes that's enough to stimulate their reflexes and get them to wake up.

Amabile: Why don't you use ammonia inhalants ?

Miller: Just because of the toxisity of ammonia, some people get really irritated with it. It can cause burns to the nasel mucosa. We don't use that stuff at all anymore.

Amabile: When a driver wakes up, it's got to be quite a shock, not only because of the impact, but he's waking up to a bunch of unfamiliar faces. How do you handle that ?

Miller: That's why we have one guy maintaining a stabilization on the driver's helmet and neck, to make sure that if he does come around quick, he won't jerk his neck around and maybe cause further injury.

Amabile: Did you guys have to use that breathing tube on any drivers at Indy in 1990 ?

Miller: Yeah, we used it during rookie orientation when Steve Barclay crashed. We had to put a tube through his nose and into his lungs, while he was pinned in the car. The car was laying on its side against the concrete wall, with the wheels off. There was no way to move it out. So when we got to the scene he was not breathing at all. We had to insert the tube down to his trachea, which was basically breathing for him until we got him to breath on his own. We went ahead and just had the helicopter land on the track and take him directly down to Methodist Hospital.

Amabile: I've talked to drivers who have crashed and were unconscious and they mentioned that they were minus one uniform.

Miller: Sometimes we've got to get into a driver's chest if they're unconscious. We don't want to manipulate the neck or the upper body, so we have to cut the suit off. We try to unzip it first, but if the zippers are snagged or anything like that we end up cutting it off. Usually we can unzip it and just cut through the underwear, unless they're really hurt bad. Then once we get him out of the car, we'll go ahead and cut the whole suit off and put the shock pants on whether they need them or not.

Amabile: What are shock pants ?

Miller: It's a military anti-shock support trouser. It sits on both legs and up to the diaphram of the chest. It inflates with air and kind of puts a terential pressure on, so if there's any internal bleeding, it acts as an external tamponod, where it's like putting pressure on a cut. It will tamponod it long enough to get him to the hospital, stabilize his blood pressure and have the surgeons take a look at him. The shock pants were developed by the military in the 1940's for the World War II pilots, because they kept passing out with the increased G forces. When the plane would go into these awesome dives, the trousers would pump up and cause a real big resistance in the lower extremities, to keep all of the blood that's usually shunted out of their chest, up into their chest and brain so that they wouldn't pass out. The fighter pilots also wear them. It's the same thing that they do on the street now.

Amabile: If the driver is pinned in the car, who does the actual extrication ?

Miller: The safety crew does while we assist in keeping the patient stable and making sure the vital signs are okay. We make sure that the neck doesn't get moved.

Amabile: The Speedway doctors have the advantage of reviewing the accident on closed circuit T.V. How does that help the safety crews ?

John Miller talks by radio with Speedway doctors after arriving at the accident scene. (Ron Weaver photos)

Miller and crew help a dazed Emerson Fittipaldi get out of his car after this turn three accident in 1987.

39

Miller: They 'll replay the accident, and at the same time they'll monitor what we're doing on the track. We're in contact with Henry Bock during the whole time. They review the impact and the mechanism of injury while they keep an eye on us and what we report. Then they kind of determine what they want to do, whether it's going to be a person who they want to ship directly out that won't even go to the infield hospital, or whether the driver will go to the infield hospital to be evaluated. If there's any kind of change in the level of consciousness, they eventually go down to Methodist to be checked out. After the driver is taken care of, we work on the track to get it opened up for the race or practice.

Amablle: If that means pushing a broom, does that mean that you're out there pushing a broom with everybody else ?

Miller: Yeah, pushing a broom, putting asphalt in the track, making sure that all of the parts and little bolts or whatever to get it race ready again.

Amablle: I guess that sometimes you need someone who's good on a broom rather than a paramedic.

Miller: Yeah, that's true. You get on a broom and start throwing oil dry.

Amablle: Once the driver is in the ambulance going back to the hospital, what are the procedures once he's in the ambulance ?

Miller: Once he's in the ambulance, there's a paramedic in the back that rides in with the driver. We can afford to let one paramedic go to the hospital now. We have three medics now. We used to have only two up until 1990. There has to be at least two paramedics on the track at all times, one at each end of the track. So we can afford to let one go to the hospital if it's a bad case.

Doctor Henry Bock has been the Speedway medical director since 1982. Dr. Bock took over as director after the death or Dr. Thomas Hanna, whom the Hanna Emergency Medical Center is named after. In normal life, Dr. Bock practices emergency medicine at the Methodost Trauma Center in Indianapolis. Dr. Bock heads a staff of 25 nurses and 10 physicians who are ready to personally resume the medical procedures once a driver arrives at the Hanna Medical Center.

Rick Amablle: John Miller mentioned that after an accident the doctors review the crash and monitor the paramedics. What goes on at the hospital during this time ?

Dr. Henry Bock: We do review the accident, but in most cases we do not have to do that because it's obvious as to what happened. The reason why T.V. is helpful for us is that it gives us a jump in preparing for probably worse scenarios than better scenarios. If we get an indication that somebody may be severely injured, not only does it give us a chance to prepare a little bit better, but also we can alert the people downtown at the Methodist Trauma Center which is the ultimate receiving point for our severely injured people. All that time and the jump that we get on it is very important as to what happens with the driver in taking care of and treating his injuries. That's why that helps us a lot. In routine things, it doesn't really give us much of an idea. The one thing that we use it a lot for however, is to see if the driver is unconscious, because that puts us into a different mind set. It lets us know, at least in most cases, that driver is probably going to go down to Methodist and be observed and reviewed and have some further diagnostic procedures done to make sure that he did not suffer any kind of head injury.

Amablle: Once the driver arrives at the infield hospital, what kind of exam do you put him through ?

Dr. Bock: The infield hospital's function is to further assess the driver's needs. Particularly to assess those needs that center around the driver's ability to breathe or take care of himself in the defensive posture. Once we determine that the driver, if he does appear to be injured, is safe enough that he will make the trip down to the trauma center without any further injury to himself, then he's out of there. So we're merely a stopping off point to make sure that the driver is supported, particularly that his airway is supported, that he can make it downtown. For the drivers that need no further evaluation or need not go to the Methodist Hospital, those drivers we look over pretty carefully for bumps and bruises and things that they may not realize that they have at first. The driver really is not always aware of little bumps and bruises that he or she may not have that the next day turn out to be big bumps and bruises. That's not unique to race car drivers, we see that everyday in emergency medicine. Drivers that were in automobile wrecks and feel pretty good, and then the next morning wake up and can't get out of bed. We want to make sure before we clear that driver to go back out and get back into the car, that there's not something that he's either feeling or we're missing.

Complete with helipad, the HEMC was built shortly after Tony Hulman purchased the track. (J. Haines photo)

Inside the Hanna Emergency Medical Center during raceday.

Amabile: After a driver has had an accident, he's usually walking around like a stick man for a few days. Drivers always feel sore for a few days, but I've talked to some who said that they still had sore spots like two weeks later.

Dr. Bock: Sure, those are really judgement calls on the part of the medical team. We determine if that drivers okay to get back into a car and drive again. We are very careful and very cognizant that the driver doesn't endanger himself by getting back in the car too soon, but endanger those others that are on the race track with him.

Amabile: You have all of the driver's medical history on computer file right ?

Dr. Bock: Yes, it's the pertinent information about their health status, whether they're on any medicines, whether they've had previous injuries and those kinds of things.

Amabile: When you check out a driver after an accident, what kind of heart rate do they usually have?

Dr. Bock: It varies of course. Drivers for the most part are in very good physical condition, so they have very low heart rates, reflecting that they are in good physical condition. You can probably put yourself in their place. If you were traveling 200 mph plus and suddenly run into a concrete wall, to say the least it's going to excite you somewhat. For the most part, by the time they get to us, most of them are pretty well under control and pretty well slowed down again.

Amabile: What kind of fan injuries do you usually get on race day ?

Dr. Bock: Mostly minor injuries that fans suffer from trying to have too good of a time. I guess that's the best way of putting it. Most are the same kinds of injuries that you would see at a carnival or a picnic area. The thing that we try to guard against the most and try to at least anticipate are people that have heart problems and serious problems such as that. Those are the people that we're really concerned about. Most people even if they would break one of their arms or their legs, don't need any kind of immediate care even though they do need to go to the hospital and get fixed. It's the heart attack people that we really try to tune our system to and plan ahead for.

Amabile: Would you like to throw anything else in which might be interesting ?

Dr. Bock: I think that the most interesting thing is the advancements that car designers have made in protecting the drivers, as well as the people that make safety equipment. There's a lot of things that you can do in designing the car, providing the driver with safety equipment, providing a safety team and training people to take care of them should they have an accident. But there are cases of course where the damage is just too great. Those are the things that we can't do anything about. In the 20 or so years that I've been involved with professional automobile racing, I'm pleased that most of the time, energy and money spent on racing, is spent to assure the safety of the drivers and the fans. I think that speaks very well of the sport. There may not be another sport out there that stresses safety as much as we do.

41

Inside Lola Cars-1991

The 1991 Lola is a logical development of the highly sucessful 1990 model which won 12 of the 16 races in 1990, including Indianapolis and the National Championship. As usual, the Lola can accomodate a Chevrolet, Cosworth or Judd engine. In addition, 1991 will see the debut of a chassis that is designed specifically around the Buick V-6 engine. This is a significant advantage because Buick customers always had to rely on older second-hand chassis in the past. The Buick version will appear in full Super Speedway trim only to take full advantage of the Buick horsepower, and the relative compactness of the engine.

Under the direction of Lola proprietor Eric Broadley, chief engineer Bruce Ashmore and company have instituted few changes to the '91 model. Most of the changes are small in detail to further enhance performance, serviceability and reliability. When CART decided to legalize the use of a full carbon fiber tub, Lola took the conservative approach and stuck to the traditional aluminum honeycomb lower section. The composite sections of the monocoque are manufactured in state-of-the-art pre-preg tools and cured in a nitrogen-pressure autoclave. This process increases the strength of the chassis and results in a smooth finish to make painting easy. This is significant because carbon fiber is difficult to paint without having to add extra coats of paint to achieve a smooth texture. Extra paint means extra weight which of course is a sin in the racing industry. The lower section of the monocoque has been widened to accept a fuel cell designed to ensure that the center of gravity of the fuel load remains as low as possible at all times. By lowering the center of gravity, less weight shifts in the upper part of the chassis which results in better handling.

The cockpit was enlarged to accomodate the varied shapes and sizes of the many Lola drivers. This was made possible by revising the front mechanical lay-out which made more room for the driver's legs and knees. Indeed, drivers who first tested the 1990 model griped that their shins and knees were rubbing up against the inner bulkheads and steering rack. Shoulder and elbow room was also increased. The mechanics haven't been forgotten in the new design: accessibility of front and rear components such as springs, dampers, anti- roll bars and inner suspension mountings.

In addition to impoving the overall aerodynamics, the front wings have been redesigned to decrease pitch sensitivity. This means that the front wings will not be as sensitive to minor adjustments such as one degree. By changing the front wing angle, the car will not react as drastically. Before, if there was a small change in angle, there was a big difference in the car's overall handling. The rear wing was changed from a three-element design, to a more elaborate five- elem-

Lola Cars, located in Huntingdon, England, about 60 miles north of London. (Rick Amabile photo)

ent pattern for increased downforce. The rear suspension now allows a greater degree of adjustment to increase performance. The air jacking system was also revised to provide a quicker and more level lifting method.

Particular attention was paid to the cooling system. As a result, the '91 model features a revised engine/gearbox cooling system. The rear uprights are now fully vented to provide increased brake and hub cooling under severe racing conditions.

As of the spring of 1991, a total of 40 chassis were sold. Dick Simon Racing was the first to take delivery in December of 1990. The 1991 Lola costs $315,000, without any spare parts or the road course kit set up. The car is sold in either the speedway set up or the road course set up. If you purchase the speedway set up, and want to convert the car over to the road course set up, the kit is around $40,000. The exact price depends on the exchange rate of the British pound to the American dollar. The Lola/ P.I. Black Box option costs an additional $33,000 for the dash display only. By the time you buy the wiring harnesses and other components that complete the system, it costs around $45,000 per car. This does not include spares and additional sets of wheels. A set of four dome (flush surface) wheels costs around $6,000.

Over the last decade, it has become increasingly apparent that Indy car racing has become an engineering war. But if it's a war, then who are the commanders ? In today's world racing technology, it is pretty safe to say that the chassis designers are the real commanders. The officials are supposed to be the leaders in this area, but we have all witnessed how some of their decisions have resulted in failure.

Bruce Ashmore is the chief designer for Lola Car's Indy car project. If there was to be one individual that held the highest post in the office of Indy car technology, Bruce could very well be the man. The youthful Ashmore was once the protege of Nigel Bennett, who left Lola to join Penske Racing in 1987. With Lola outnumbering its competition by almost 9 to 1, I wanted to sit down and discuss how a new car evolves, and also the present and future of the modern Indy car.

Rick Amabile: When did the actual design process begin on the 1991 Lola ?

Bruce Ashmore: We start thinking about the next car as soon as we finish the last one. The '90 was finished at the end of November 1989; that's when we started working on the '91 but we're doing it alongside the development of the '90 car. So during '89, we had ideas that we wanted to put on the car, but ran out of time. So we add all of the answers from the development in '89. So during November-December '89, we were already developing pieces for the '90 car, but alongside that there's further reaching changes that we can't do to the '90 that we want to take a little further from what we've developed so far, so there are our '91 ideas. These were somethings that we couldn't physically change: the shape of the tub or the shape of the concept layout of the car. So that's really your '91 development that's going on in December of '89. Hard design of the '91 really started after Indy in 1990. That's when we started doing schemes. The actual schemes for the design of the components started in May of 1990. Then the detailed designs of the pieces started in the end of June, and then it goes on from there.

Amabile: How many people are on the design team?

Ashmore: There's myself who runs the project, I have two assistants doing the detail design. I do the concept, they do the design of the schemes of the car. Then we have three draftsmen who draw all of the components of the car from the assistant's sketches. Then we have a CAD engineer who does all of the machine drawings of the bodywork. All body work drawings come straight from the CAD. The CAD engineer takes the schemes from the models and makes full size surface drawings of the car, then that gets cut with a direct link down to a router, which the bucks are made from.

Amabile: Who actually builds the bucks and molds for the cars ?

Ashmore: We have two full-time model makers. We have a model aerodynamicist who trains everybody such as I do. I run the aerodynamic program but he makes sure the models get built and get to the wind tunnel.

Amabile: When did the actual building process of the 1991 car start ?

Ashmore: The bucks and molds were built in July - August of '90. We started putting the first chassis together in October. Then in November we started bolting everything on to the chassis. Then at the end of November, the beginning of December, we have a finished car.

Amabile: Who determines who gets the first car ?

Ashmore: It goes by whoever puts down the first deposit. The little teams are usually the first ones to get the first car. There's a bit of superstition behind getting the first car. The little teams haven't got anything to lose, so they always ask for the first car. The larger teams don't really want it.

Amabile: Yeah, it's pretty obvious when Carl Haas doesn't get the first car.

Ashmore: He doesn't get the first car because he tries to put the customer first. He wears two hats. He'll take about the fourth or fifth car. The first car thing came from years ago. The first car used to be the prototype. It probably had lots of holes in the wrong places and the wrong size bolts. It was a bit of a nasty car. Everything is productionized now, so we don't have a prototype. So everything is proven in the mockup stages. So really the first car is as good as all of the other cars, but there's still the superstition that has hung over. So it's not a problem anymore. It gives one of the smaller teams a jump in the line up.

Amabile: How's the '91 car technically different than the previous models ?

Ashmore: Every car is based off of the previous car. The '91 looks a lot different from the '89, but it's essentially the same car. Conceptually it's the same weight distribution, the same geometry, the same stiffness and the same wheel rates. It's just that the aerodynamics are slightly different. It's still the same concept of aerodynamics but everything's a different shape.

Amabile: So the '91 is basically the same mechanically ?

The fine art of setting up an Indy car requires precise communication between the driver and engineer. Ashmore also serves as a set up engineer for Newman/Haas Racing. (Doug Wendt)

44

Ashmore: Right. It just looks different. Next year's car will look similar in some areas and different in other areas. Every car is a development of the previous car, it's just that sometimes the changes are on the outside and sometimes the changes are on the inside.

Amabile: What took the Indy cars so long to come into using the six speed gearbox ?

Ashmore: The engine power band is wider on an Indy car engine than it is on a Formula One engine. So it was just deemed not necessary in the past. But as soon as one team did it, like Penske, then they had an advantage. So we had to do it to catch up. When you go for a development idea, you have to look at it and question whether or not it will make a gain. Because of the wide power band, we could always make a case that it wasn't going to be a gain. It's an expensive thing to make and try.

Amabile: What are the advantages of the six speed gearbox ?

Ashmore: It just keeps the engine in its powerband for more of the lap. That's the idea behind it.

Amabile: Does Lola design its own gearboxes ?

Ashmore: Yeah, we design the gearbox. We have the cases made by an outside contractor, then we have them delivered over to Hewland and they make all of the gears and shafts. So the gears are their gears and they 're primarily their design, but we also designed it to suit the six speeds, drop gears and ring and pinions. Hewland does all of the assembly. They make all of the steel parts in the gearbox.

Amabile: How many people does Lola employ now ?

Ashmore: About 150. The majority is in the design department. There's about 26 in the design department. We have four projects: Indy cars, Formula One, Group C and Formula 3000. The Indy car is the biggest project.

Amabile: Do you participate in the design of the Formula One car at all ?

Ashmore: No. There's four project leaders, which I'm one of them. We have meetings every month to go over ideas and just cross flow the ideas. So I guess we each play a part in each others project. If I find out something on my project, then I suggest it to the other projects. If it's an idea that can work on every car, then it's incorporated into each design.

Amabile: Have you been running the project ever since Nigel Bennett left in 1987 ?

Ashmore: Yeah, from the middle of '87. So I did the '88 car, which was a development of the '87 car.

Amabile: Where do you guys wind tunnel test ?

Ashmore: At the Cranfield Institute of Technology in England It's like a university. We also do all of the crash tests there.

Amabile: How many wind tunnel hours went into the '91 car ?

Ashmore: We're in the wind tunnel for about five days per month.

Amabile: So like five, eight hours days ?

Ashmore: Oh, no, we start at eight in the morning and finish about ten at night. We book the wind tunnel for two weeks per month, then we divide that up between the four projects. That's throughout the whole year. The wind tunnel alternates between next year's car, the current car and doing current car development. So we have three or four models that we're taking over there all the time.

Amabile: So really, you guys were thinking about the '92 car just before Christmas 1990.

Ashmore: Yeah, that's when we start the '92.

Amabile: Do you think that they will ban ground effects in '92 or '93 ?

Ashmore: That's a really big misconception. You can't ban ground effects. Every racing car is a ground effect car. A Formula One car is a ground effect car. Ground effects means that it creates downforce in the proximity of the car to the ground. That always happens.

Amabile: I mean eliminating the tunnels and going flat bottomed.

Ashmore: Well they 're talking about it, but it would be a big disaster if they do. I don't think they will go flat bottomed.

Amabile: If they did go flat bottomed, how much do you think it would slow the cars down ?

Ashmore: I really can't see the big teams slowing down. It will slow the little teams down. The flat bottom area produces a lot of downforce. That's another misconception. A Formula One car has the same downforce as an Indy car. They have a little kick up at the rear of the car, but it's getting flatter all the time. The flat bottom uses very low pressures. It's just that it's pitch sensitive so you have to spend a lot of time controlling the pitch sensitivity. That's where all the development is, which the big teams in this series would latch onto straight away. So the only thing flat bottoms will do is hurt the little teams. It will make a bigger divide between the big teams and the little teams.

Amabile: So would there probably be a lot more crashes ?

Ashmore: Oh yeah. You saw that in 1990 at Indy when they went from the ten inch underwing exit, down to an eight inch exit. It makes it more pitch sensitive. If we go away from that and go totally flat it will be even more pitch sensitive. But the big teams don't crash, and the big teams don't slow down.

Amabile: Then are the little teams the guinea pigs so to speak ?

Ashmore: No. They are if the rules people don't treat the rules right, yes. That's why I think that this series is the way it's been so far, by chipping away a little bit, it's been very sensible.

Amabile: Okay, so all of the critics and old-timers who say "they should go to flat bottoms like back in the olden days and put the driver back into it". Do they know what they 're talking about ?

Ashmore: No. It would actually put less of the driving into it if they were to go flat bottomed. It becomes more of an engineering exercise then a driving exercise. It's a misconception. They think they 're taking the downforce away but they 're not. The downforce stays the same, it's just harder to control.

Amabile: Are you still learning about ground effects like you were maybe five of ten years ago ?

Ashmore: Yeah, we don't stop learning because every time we change something in the wind tunnel, it answers one question and asks two more. Then we go in and answer those two questions and it asks two more. It just goes on and on, it never stops. The job lists going into the tunnel get longer.

Amabile: Lets go into the wings a little bit. How much downforce do the wings produce ? How much extra downforce does a small wicker bill add, say on a super-speedway wing ?

Ashmore: A small wicker will add about 30 pounds extra. The road course read wings generate about 2000 pounds at 200 mph. A smaller speedway wing produces about 400 pounds at 200 mph. A front road course wing is about 500 pounds total.

Amabile: What about total downforce ?

Ashmore: The '90 car about 4,500 pounds at 200 mph, or about 3,800 pounds at 180 mph. That's for the road course set-up. The speedway set-up, like at Indy, is about 3,200 pounds at 200 mph.

Amabile: What do you think an Indy car will look like in the year 2010 ? I mean you probably think about it in the back of your mind a little ?

Ashmore: Oh, it's hard. I can't see that far ahead.

Amabile: Do you ever wish that they would change the rules, maybe enclose the cockpits to help clean up the airflow ?

Ashmore: Oh, no. I think that the rule process in this series is very good. We just chip away a little each year. Chip away at the safety or the speed. It keeps us on our toes. It keeps the speeds up to a point where it's exciting for the spectators, but not outrageously dangerous for the drivers. I mean it is a dangerous sport, so we're not going to make it totally safe, but we can cut out the unnecessary risks.

Many drivers welcomed the 1991 Lola as it has increased leg and shoulder room. Hall / VDS driver John Andretti compares the 1991 chassis to the 1990 model which he first tested after signing his new contract.

Rick Amabile: How does the '91 car feel different than the '90 ?

John Andretti: When you talk about feel, the cars are not identicle. It's just a matter of finding good balance on both. When you achieve good balance, you get the cars to be very similar. One car feels better on an oval,

and the other feels better on a road course. I think that it's basically finding the better balance on each car. They 're very similar in feel when you get right down to it.

Amabile: Is the ride about the same ?

Andretti: Yeah, they just have a little bit different wheel rates and things. I think the '91 has a lower rear roll center. Once you start figuring out the little things that it likes and doesn't like, you start making it a better car than the '90.

Amabile: How does the '91 cockpit feel ?

Andretti: It's quite a bit different the way you fit in it. It's an all carbon (fiber) cockpit, where the side panels are carbon instead of aluminum. I like the '91 cockpit better because it fits me a little bit better. They made it bigger in the hips, but it's tighter in the elbow area. I think that it's just the way I sit in the car. The fire extinguisher bottle isn't beneath your legs anymore, it's behind your lower back. That gives you a lot better angle in your thighs going under the bulkhead. On the '90 car, my legs go almost straight up in the air. You sit down on the bottom of the car, but then there's this huge hump for the fire extinguisher.

Amabile: I thought that they put the fire extinguisher underneath the driver's legs to keep him from moving forward under braking ?

Andretti: With the size of the fire extinguisher, and the size of the car, they 're running out of space up there. For us little guys, our feet don't go too far down in there. The '91 car is much more comfortable in that area. You have to remember that I just came out of the '90 Porsche. That car was built around Teo (Fabi) and myself. We both have size 6 1/2 feet.. That car was very tight. So compared to that, the '91 Lola is like driving a tractor-trailer rig in that area! There's much more leg room in the '91 then there is in the '90, just because they took out the fire extinguisher. It helps your legs stay lower so your shins aren't up into the steering rack.

Amabile: Is the suspension response about the same?

Andretti: Any time you test a new chassis, it seems to be more responsive because it just doesn't have a year of wear and tear on it. The torsional (twisting motion) ridgitity of a car always changes. Carbon fiber makes the car retain more of its ridgidity after a season. The '90 car that we have is still very responsive. The only thing that you notice is that a little change on the '91, may not be as responsive on the '90. Four of five years ago, the cars weren't very responsive at the end of the season. I think that carbon fiber technology has come along way so the cars remain more consistant. The old aluminum riveted tubs are terrible that way. I've driven a GTP Porsche which was all rivets, you could change 1,000 pounds on the springs and sometimes you wouldn't even notice the change.

(See page 74)

Penske Racing

Roger Penske trimmed down his team to two drivers for 1991. For the first time in years, the Penske team will share the same colors. Drivers Rick Mears and Emerson Fittipaldi are probably the most respected on the circuit. Penske Racing employs an immense staff of 128 people. 58 work at the shop base in Reading, Pennsylvania, while the other 70 personnel are employed at Penske's design and fabrication shop in Poole, England.

Being the largest team in Indy car racing includes the monumental task of accommodating so many people. Tim Lombardi is the team coordinator. Tim is responsible for making sure that all of the team personnel and equipment get from point A to point B in an orderly fashion. When Penske Racing hits the road, it brings two transporters each carrying two race cars, a pit/fuel truck which carries a 500 gallon methanol tank, pumps, pit equipment, golf carts, fuel hoses etc. Because Penske uses Mobil One products, they are not eligible for Valvoline's fuel service. The pit/fuel truck also tows a kitchen trailer which prepares meals for the hospitality trailer. Over the winter of 1990, the Marlboro Racing hospitality trailer was taken over by Penske and remodeled. The team used to have a separate bus, but that got transferred down to Penske's new NASCAR operation.

When it comes to the average race weekend, Lombardi arranges the travel plans. " On a normal race weekend, we take along 50 to 60 people. It just depends on the event." Travel arrangements are booked well in advance. " Hotels are booked about a year in advance. We have to do ours quite a ways in advance because we're such a big group, it's tough because the cities that we go to are generally jammed. So we have to plan well in advance in order to get the block of rooms that we need. For most events, we rent a block of 30 to 45 rooms, depending on where we're at." Indianapolis for that matter was never really meant to be an average event. "For the month of May we rent about 20 to 25 rooms for the entire month, up until race weekend, at the airport Dillon Inn. Race weekend, Penske Corporation takes the entire (131 room) hotel. Out of that, the race team will use up about 60 or 70 rooms with the remainder going to to rest of the corporation. We try to book air fares far enough in advance so that we can take advantage of some low air fairs. That doesn't always work out because with the way racing is, you 're always changing plans every time you turn around." Roger Penske, who lives in Red Bank, New Jersey and maintains his offices in Detroit, flies in his own private Citation III airplane.

On March 10, 1991, the Indy car set traveled down under to Australia for the season opener. Packaging all of the cars and equipment for the trip in Formula One style was a new adventure for Indy car teams. "We loaded everything on flat pallets. Each pallet was about ten feet long and six feet wide. Because we took three cars over, we were provided a total of six pallets, three for the cars, and three for equipment. We put about 5,000 pounds of gear on the equipment pallets. It took a lot of planning. We taped off a section the size of a pallet on the floor then measured all of our containers to make sure that everything would fit when we got to L. A. to load it on the plane."

Five cars were built for the 1991 season. Penke Racing rotates a total of 25 Chevrolet engines which are maintained by the team's engine shop, headed by Karl Kainhofer, who has been with Penske since 1966. Richard Buck and Rick Rinaman are the respective chief mechanics for Mears and Fittipaldi. In addition to chief engineer Nigel Bennett, set up engineers include Peter Gibbons (Mears) and Grant Newberry (Fitipaldi).

In the late 1970's and early 1980's, Penske was in the business of building cars for any team who wanted one. This philosophy did not survive it into the 1990's. Lombardi explains why; "We have 70 people over in England just to build our five or six cars per year. If we were to get into a production line, we'd have to sacrifice the quality of work that we do in order to mass produce a customer car."

An engine technician tends to one of Penske Racing's engines in the engine room which is under the same roof as the race shop. (Jim Cutler photo)

Patrick Racing International

Patrick Racing International is owned by a combination of U.E. "Pat" Patrick, Jim McGee, and Mo Nunn. After securing Miller Brewing Company as their main sponsor in 1990, Patrick later signed Danny Sullivan, who was the odd man out at the Penske stable after the conclusion of the 1990 season. Sullivan, probably the most marketable driver on the circuit, was a breath of fresh air for both Patrick and engine supplier Alfa Romeo. Team manager and Vice President Jim McGee was obviously very pleased to obtain the services of Mr. Sullivan. " I could tell from our first test at the beginning of the year that he's really a great one. He's very professional, and a natural leader. In a program such as we're running, you need a driver with a lot of leadership qualities and he certainly has that. He's very marketable and I think that the image for Alfa is very good, because right now they 're really the only organization that's challenging Chevrolet."

1991 will see some changes in the organization of the team. Mike Hull is now the chief mechanic with former chief Joe Flynn moving over to shop manager.

Pat Patrick, who seemed to lose interest in racing over the past few years and ultimately sold his original team to Chip Ganassi, has had a renewed interest in the business. McGee has observed Patrick's restored enthusiasm, " The new Alfa deal really revitalized him. I mean, I've never seen him like he is right now. He's into the racing 100 percent. There's no talk of backing off or retirement. Pat and I have had a really great relationship for the past twelve years and I feel very comfortable with our program. We've got a big challenge that we're trying to put together in 1991".

On the engineering side, Patrick's set up engineer is Steve Newey, who was formerly with the Arrows Formula One team and Galles/Kraco Racing. Patrick, like other teams has set up a shop in England over the winter of 1990 -1. "We have a small shop over there that we're using strictly for wind tunnel work. We have our models, engineers and model makers over there. They just work on improving the aerodynamic model of the car. We don't build anything over there, it's strictly a wind tunnel program." The question is, why wind tunnel test in England rather than here in America ? "There's no good wind tunnels over here with rolling roads" (which has a moving surface under the model) McGee explains, " Wind tunnels are very important as far as the data that you get back. If you don't get back the proper data, then all it does is cost you money. Over there, they 've been doing it for so many years that they have established a good baseline. Coming over here and starting from scratch, you 'd have to spend probably six months to a year before you really got back accurate information out of a tunnel".

Perhaps the most confidential side of the team deals with the Alfa Romeo engine program. Alfa has been working on a five valve engine head since 1989. "There's a new engine, we first ran it in early 1991. I think that it's going to be a surprise to everybody. There are modifications that are going to come along over the 1991 season. We had modifications for Phoenix and Long Beach, and another for Indianapolis and another after that." But why all of the secrecy ? " They (Alfa Romeo) just feel that why give away what you 're running ? It's hard to tell what they are running because you can't see it." All of the effort that Alfa Romeo is putting into their Indy car program dictates that they are pouring millions of dollars toward future competitiveness. Millions which may include the salary of Danny Sullivan. There's little doubt that Alfa will soon see the victory circle.

Patrick Racing is located on Gasoline Alley street, just a few miles south of the Indianapolis Motor Speedway. Patrick employs a total of 38 people, 8 of which are based in England. This number does not include the team of Alfa Romeo people that are assigned to the project.

Galles / Kraco Racing

After winning the National Championship in 1990 with Al Unser, Jr., Galles / Kraco Racing is back in full force for 1991. When Rick Galles teamed with Kraco boss Maurice Kraines in 1990, it presented the additional challenge of running a two driver team. Two drivers are not always favorable for some owners, but Galles / Kraco overcame the obstacles to become a better unit. Team manager, Barry Green, who has been with Kraines since 1986, explains the extra effort to run both Al Unser, Jr. and Bobby Rahal, " Just because of the sheer size of the team, you probably double the amount of everyday problems that you normally have. When you have such good sponsors and owners like we have, then you can afford to pay good money for good people. We have so many experienced people on this team. They all know motor racing, both the good points and the bad points, that reduces the number of problems that you normally have, just through the experience of the team." One of the other problems that a two car team can present is inner team competition. " On the race track, it's one team against the other ", Green relates. " But up until that point, the only way that we won the Championship last year was because we worked as one team. There were so many times that Bobby helped Al Jr. win or do well in a race, as Al Jr. helped Bobby. One weekend it would be one driver helping the other and the next weekend, just for some reason, it would turn out to be just the opposite. Bobby would find something that worked and we would put it on Al's car and away he went. Then the next weekend, Al would find something that we'd put on Bobby's car, and away he would go. I was very surprised that the two car team concept worked as well as it has in that area."

One of the benefits that Galles /Kraco enjoys is having two veteran team owners. " They understand what money it takes, and that's the name of the game. They go out and get the sponsors and they know what our goals are as far as the budget. They 're prepared to support the team with any short falls, if there are any. The best part about working with Rick Galles and Maury Kraines is that they 've both been down the road where they haven't been winning any races, and they don't want any more of that. They just look at what it's going to take as far as budget-wise, and they get the job done." Galles/Kraco rotates a total of 21 Chevrolet engines, which are prepared by VDS engines.

Similar to the Truesports team, Galles/Kraco have also been working on building their own chassis. The car is being built by Galmer engineering in England. Galmer is a joint venture, between Rick Galles and former March engineer Allan Mertens, which employs 17 people. Galmer is trying to debut its car at some point during the 1991 season, but the project seems to be taking a back seat to the successful Lola chassis as the team has purchased five 1991 Lolas. Galles/ Kraco operates out of a 45,000 square foot shop in Albuquerque, New Mexico and employs a total of 38 people. The team has been joined by former Shierson Racing engineer John Dick. Owen Snyder is the chief mechanic for Al Unser, Jr. while Jim Prescott tends to Bobby Rahal. The team will try to capture its first Indy 500 victory and second National Championship in 1991. This goal will not be an easy task as Green comments, " Our main goal is to try to win another Championship again. We all know that it is going to take a better effort than we put in last year."

Hall/VDS Racing

1991 will see a reborn entry into Indy car racing for both Jim Hall and VDS Racing. Jim Hall, the man who introduced modern ground effects to Indy car racing in1979 with the famous 2K Chaparral, teamed with Franz Weis of VDS Engines in the fall of 1990 to create Hall / VDS Racing. Weis along with Count Rudy van der Straten (of Belgium) were formally owners of VDS Racing which campaigned an Indy car effort in 1983 and early 1984, before folding up their team at Indianapolis in 1984. VDS Engines, which is owned by Weis and Van der Straten, rebuild engines for various Indy car teams. VDS prepared engines have won Indianapolis three times and the CART National Championship five times.

Over the last eight years, Jim Hall has been tending to other business interests and privately restoring some of the old Chaparral race cars. When Hall / VDS

Racing announced their plans for 1991, one of the bombshells that was announced was that they had obtained the wealthy Pennzoil sponsorship. Jim Hall II, the team's president, explains how this new venture came to be, " The opportunity arose between dad and Pennzoil and he got together with Franz and Count Van der Straten and myself and set up the team." Jim Hall II was involved with his father's operation in the early 1980's, then started his own go-cart school in California which is still in operation. Pennzoil formally sponsored Jim Hall Racing from 1979 until Hall's departure from Indy car racing at the end of the 1982 season. Jim Hall has won Indianapolis twice; first in 1978 with Al Unser, and then in 1980 with Johnny Rutherford.

When the new team was announced, they were honored to be granted a Chevrolet engine. "Dad has had a wonderful realationship with Chevrolet in the past and Franz has done a great job rebuilding the Indy Chevys since 1987." "They knew that we would be a top of the line team and that we were going to have a top of the line driver, and a great sponsor. We applied for it and they made their decision." The top line driver is, of course, Porsche refugee John Andretti.

Larry Curry, former crew chief of Vince Granatelli Racing, serves as chief mechanic and team manager. The set-up engineering aspect of the team is a combined effort between Jim Hall, Larry Curry and engineer Chuck Matthews. Hall / VDS employs 20 people and operates out of a 10,000 square foot shop located in Midland, Texas which is about 300 miles west of Dallas.

Dick Simon Racing

Former driver Dick Simon is putting forward his strongest effort ever. Primary sponsor Amway has increased its sponsorship which helped secure Chevrolet engines for driver Scott Brayton. Simon was overjoyed to finally get a competitive engine program. "Both Amway and Hoechst Celanese increased their sponsorship in an effort to allow us to concentrate more on Scott. I think that some of the things that entered into Chevrolet's decision was our decision to make a major effort to put Scott up front ."

The increase in sponsorship is finally giving Simon the resources that he has always sought after. "Amway has increased their sponsorship budget, year after year, to where we're strong enough that we're now having the program that I've always dreamed of. We're not a Penske operation by any means, but it's a dream come true for us. We're just not used to having the dollars that the major teams are used to having. Although the dollars that we have is still a fraction of theirs, it's far more than we ever had. So it's allowing us to have better test equipment, more research and development equipment, better overall equipment altogether. Like last year, we used to stretch the turbochargers. We'd run 1,200 miles on them instead of 800 before rebuilding them. We'd try to stretch this and stretch that. This year our program is budgeted to have more replacement of parts at an earlier date and things like that. That's what money does for you."

Simon also has a reputation of hiring new drivers and giving them a chance. In this modern era of racing, some inexperienced drivers have big sponsors that back them. Some observers have criticized Simon for hiring drivers whose only recommendation was backing by a major corporation. Simon defends himself and sets the record straight: "We don't do it for money for (wife) Diane and I, we're doing it toward increasing the competitiveness of the team. So when we take a driver in like we did last year with Hiro Matsushita for example, budget-wise, it really wasn't enough to do the program as strong as we tried to do it. So helping Hiro is two fold; number one, I think that he's a good driver, number two, I feel that given the opportunity as the top drivers, he would be competitive. A lot of people look at Hiro's 1990 season and don't get too impressed, but they don't understand that he was driving an '89 with the inserts and all of that. Given the right equipment, I think that he will open a few eyes. Sometimes I'll help a driver like Jeff Wood or Didier Theys and I could go on down the line, and people wonder why did he help this person ? A good example was Scott Pruett. When we gave him his CART rookie test and everything, I was hoping that Scott would be somebody that we could build on. So Diane and I took a gamble, we gave him three separate tests before the Long Beach race in '88. He got up to sixth place in the race when he missed a shift and scattered the engine. When you look at it from the three tests that we gave him, for the 60 thousand that we got, and the engines that he used, we lost a fortune trying to get him started but you can't look at it from that standpoint. I have no bad feeling whatsoever over the fact that we lost money because sometimes when you have to walk up to the crap table, you have to put money on the table more than once to get a return. I came from a school where nobody gave me much help, so I have a weakness for helping people. We're trying so desperately to build a winning combination, that I have felt that certain drivers would be part of that winning combination."

Dick Simon employs 22 people and will be moving from their present shop which used to be a firehouse, to a larger shop, later in 1991. Engineer David Cripps oversees the set up of the teams three 1991 Lola chassis. The team rotates a total of seven Chevrolet engines.

Newman / Haas Racing

Newman / Haas Racing employs 35 people and is based just north of Chicago. Owners Paul Newman and Carl Haas have been together in Indy Car Racing since 1983. Like any other two car team, a race weekend can become a little hectic in the area of organization. Team manager Ed Nathman explains the effort behind fielding Mario and Michael Andretti, " Teamwise, people think that you can cut corners, but you can't. You have to duplicate the team to run two cars. You need more people because you have two cars, two transporters and parts coming in all of the time. It can become a little hectic. The race weekend is the same weekend over and over again, you just go to different places. The work becomes habit. What you need the extra people for is when something doesn't go right, like if you have a crash or something. You need to build up a team like you would build a power plant, you have to build it for the maximum load. If everything goes wrong, how many people do you need? That's how many people you take to the race track. If you build a race team for when everything's going right, you could have two people on a car and they could handle it. Normally, everything runs smoothly except for that two or three times a season when there's a pretty big problem. You hire the extra people to sort of cover your ass on those weekends ."

When Michael Andretti signed on as a test driver for Team McLaren, Newman / Haas had to be a little flexible with their testing schedule. " McLaren has changed their test schedule and we adjusted ours. Michael races over here and they know that. I sent them our test schedule and they changed their schedule slightly so Michael can get there on time."

With Newman / Haas Racing having three celebrities including Paul Newman and its drivers around, work conditions can become cluttered with all kinds of autograph seekers. " It presents a problem, but we're so used to it, it's just there and we do our work. It's not a factor that's overwelming at all. You barge through the crowd and start working ". Newman / Haas hase a total of 18 Chevrolet engines which are maintained by VDS Engines.

TrueSports

When TrueSports unveiled their own 91C Indy car, it represented the first car to be built in America since Dan Gurney's Eagle program in 1985. TrueSports no doubt took a big risk in constructing their own chassis. Not only was it a competitive risk, but a financial risk as well. TrueSports joins Penske and Lola as the only manufacturers in the series. Almost every Indy car team dreams of building their own car. The obvious reason why only a few can actually do it is the tremendous amount of money it takes to build just one prototype. TrueSports has claimed that each of its three 91C chassis cost $650,000 to produce. To help save money for the project, the team ran older '89 Lolas during the 1990 season.

Simply spending vast amounts of money does not necessarily breed a successful car. Aside from past Penske failures such as the PC-12 thru PC-16 series, such teams as Shierson and Kraco have also taken trips down the unsuccessful chassis manufacturing trail. Ironically, TrueSports 91C designer Don Halliday also penned the ill-fated Kraco car in late 1985. The Kraco project got caught up in politics between Kraco and March and was tested but never raced. Halliday, a New Zealander, also had experience with the Brabham Formula One team.

The 91C was developed solely in the United States, with about half of the project actually manufactured in the States. The car was built at TrueSport's marvelous shop located in Hilliard, Ohio. Wind tunnel tests were conducted at a former U.S. Air Force wind tunnel facility at Port Columbus, about 20 minutes from the TrueSports shop. TrueSports teamed with Ohio State University to blow out the "moth balls" to re-open and refurbish the abandoned wind tunnel facility.

TrueSports followed CART's new rule of permitting an all-carbon fiber / composite monocoque tub. The tub was built by R-cubed Corp. in Salt Lake City, Utah. R-cubed specializes in work for the aerospace industry. The cockpit was basically designed around driver Scott Pruett who himself has had a hand in the cars development.

Along with Don Halliday, aerodynamacist Gary Grossenbacher and crew started working on the project around August 1989. Halliday and Grossenbacher then enlisted the help of OSU professor Dr. John Lee and his crew of students. The design team estimate that over 1,200 hours were spent in the wind tunnel.

The 91C is a very nicely designed package. Along with the all-carbon tub, the cars feature shorter sidepods than their competition and minimal frontal area. The slim and tidy engine cover flows back cleanly to connect with the transverse gearbox. The 6-speed gearbox was designed by Chris Weismann and built by Weismann at their shop in Costa Mesa, Calif. The suspension design is the rather conventional double wishbone, with pushrods operating inboard springs/ dampers. The 91C of course is powered by a further modified version of the Judd V-8 engine. The car's specifications are as follows; wheelbase: 111.5 inches, front track: 67.6 inches, rear track: 63.5 inches, overall length: 184 inches, overall width: 78.8 inches, weight: 1,550 pounds.

TrueSports was founded in 1982 by Red Roof Inns owner Jim Trueman. Trueman died of cancer in June 1986 and the team's presidency was passed on to former chief mechanic and team manager Steve Horne. Trueman's dreams were to someday win the Indy 500, win the national championship and build his own car. The 91C project marks the third and final culmination of that dream. With the advent of the new car project, TrueSports now employs over 90 full-time people. Budweiser has been the team's primary sponsor since 1985. Red Roof Inns and Conaco complete the associate sponsor lineup along with several companies that contributed their equipment and knowledge into the development of the 91C.

51   The spacious shop floor, machine and welding areas in TrueSports ultra modern facility. (TrueSports photo)

UNO / Granatelli Racing

In 1990, Bob Tezak, owner of International Games Inc., bought the Indy winning team of Doug Shierson Racing. Tezak, who is most familiar for his UNO game, had been sponsoring various Indy car teams since 1980. Tezak, a Phoenix resident, got together with Vince Granatelli, whose existing team was experiencing hard luck, and formed UNO / Granatelli Racing in late 1990. Tezak had a Chevy contract plus 1990 Indianapolis 500 winner Arie Luyendyk, and Granatelli had vast experience along with a beautiful 50,000 square foot shop. The merger seemed to be a great opportunity for both owners. Vince Granatelli explains his new partnership, "Bob lives here in Phoenix and we've been friends for a while. Arie lives out here, and Mo Nunn moved out here. We just thought that with so many of us living in Phoenix, and having such a fantastic facility here, and the fact that we all like racing but we all have to travel. It didn't make any sense to travel to different parts of the country to go to your shop. It all melted together. We could get a Chevrolet at the same time, so we just got together and made a deal."

Granatelli had been struggling to get the Buick engine competitive on the CART circuit. With CART not wanting to get into an equivilancy formula in the area of turbo boost, fielding a Buick other than at Indianapolis, proved to be a losing battle. Granatelli was certainly relieved to finally gain Chevy power, " Of course we've always wanted to be competitive, and haven't had much sucess over the past couple of years. Now with the Chevrolet engine and the same equipment as everybody else has, we don't have any excuses now."

In addition to a Chevy contract, Granatelli was also pleased to have Luyendyk on board. " It's nice to work with Arie. We've been friends for a while, so it's nice to work with him in addition to being friends."

UNO / Granatelli employs 40 people. Mo Nunn, who moved over from Patrick Racing, serves as the team's engineer. The team has pooled their sponsors together: RCA, Total Petroleum, Provimi Veal and UNO are the main sponsors.

Bettenhausen Racing

In 1990, just about every team that didn't have a Chevy applied for one. Tony Bettenhausen was one of the lucky recipients. Bettenhausen, the youngest son of the racing legend, started his own team in 1985 with the help of several associate owners. In addition to the Chevy deal, the team took delivery of a pair of Penske Chevy '90s. The team first tested their new combination in December 1990. Tony Bettenhausen was quite pleased with the Penske Chevy '90. " I've never driven the '89 Lola without the inserts in the tunnels, but there's a world of difference between that and the Penske ." Unlike some other teams with Chevy power, Bettenhausen did not have to buy the engines. " It's a lease program, not a buy. I think that all of the new teams are on the deal. I'm really not sure because I hear conflicting stories. You pay a fee at the beginning of the year and then you' re in charge of keeping the engines maintained. We've got a total of seven engines that we rotate ." When Penske Racing trimmed down to a two car effort, their engine shop had extra space and personnel to rebuild engines for three cars throughout a season. Due to this fact, Penske took on the Bettenhausen team as the third car and will be providing their services for this small team.

Along with the sale of the Penske chassis comes the option of engineering consultation, which will be provided by Tom Brown, who works for Penske Cars in England.

AMAX Coal returns as the major sponsor. AMAX Coal primarily deals in aluminum. "About 62 percent of the company profits are from aluminum."

The team is managed by veteran Paul Diatlovich with Rick Duman serving as chief mechanic. Bettenhausen Racing is based on Gasoline Alley street, across the street from Hemelgarn Racing.

Dale Coyne Racing

Dale Coyne signed drivers Randy Lewis and talented young Canadian Paul Tracy for his most serious effort ever. Tracy, the 1990 Indy Lights (ARS) champion, originally signed a testing contract with TrueSports with an option for a full time ride. When the sponsorship hunt failed, Tracy was back ride hunting and later picked up by Coyne. Lewis is sponsored by AMP and Orbit semiconductors. AMP is the worlds largest manufacturer of electronic connectors. Former driver Dale Coyne has built up his team from a tiny shoestring effort in the middle to late 1980's, to a respectable level in the 1990's. This gradual transition has taught Coyne valuable lessons on how to stretch a racing dollar. " I think that the same philosophy is there, that's why as you step up, I think that you can do more with maybe a little bit less than some of the other owners have, because you used to have to do it with nothing. You learn how to get the most with what you have. If you have a little more, you just get more out of it than hopefully someone else will. So I think that experience is invaluable. When you 've raced with hardly any money at all, as soon as you get a little money, I think that you can do a good program."

Coyne employs a crew of 15 people, some of which started as "weekend warriors". The team's base is outside of Chicago and they plan on building a larger 12,000 square foot shop later in 1991. Chief mechanic Bernie Meyers has been with Dale ever since the beginning. The two were once partners in an automotive paint business, but had to wind it down to concentrate on the racing business full time. The team has five Cosworth DFS engines.

A few years ago, other teams would snicker when Dale Coyne and crew would arrive at an Indy car race in an old motorhome and small trailer, and park it next to the other team's lavish transporters and hospitality buses. " I think that people respect what we've done, because we did it because we were racers. We didn't do it because it was a good deal, we did it because we were racers. We used to camp out in a motorhome and that's unheard of. Everybody's done that to pay their dues, but we did it in Indy car racing ! We haven't lost touch with that. We still have that old motorhome parked behind the shop. Bernie and I have this joke that if our heads ever get too big, or we get too big for our shoes, we'll just go out and lock ourselves in the old motorhome for a couple of days and all reality will set back in ."

Bayside Motorsports

Bayside Motorsports is in its third year of Indy car racing. The team, who has had Texaco sponsorship in the past, was asked by Texaco if they would give e test to rookie Jeff Andretti. Jeff was hired to complete the Texaco-Havoline-Andretti line up. Team general manager, Walter Gerber, gives his first impressions of working with Mario's youngest son, "He's a very good driver to work with, very responsive. Actually, I think that he surprised all us in his first test with us at Portland. He can respond quickly to changes, he can communicate well with the engineer and mechanics that make the changes and go out and improve his lap time. He's very quick down onto the time, never more than two laps until he's back down onto a plateau."

Bayside is owned by Bruce Levin, whose business dealings include three car dealerships, and an airline company that operates sea planes. Bayside gets its name from Levin's business ventures which once included Bayside trash disposal which was sold a few years ago.

The team operates from a 20,000 square foot shop in Redmond, Washington and employs 15 full time people. Former Kraco shop foreman Bill Eaton sees to the daily management of the team. Steve Erickson, who was formally with now defunct Porsche effort, is the team's trackside engineer. Bayside is powered by Cosworth DFS Phase II engines. The team applied for and was denied Chevy power for 1991. " We came close, but politics got involved ." Gerber explains, "There were just too many things that were against us. Hopefully, the new DFS Phase II Cosworth will be just as competitive."

Euromotorsports

Euromotorsports has stepped up its involvement in Indy car racing. In addition to running two cars in '91, the team has moved into a brand new 14,000 square foot shop in Indianapolis. The team signed two new drivers: Canadian John Jones and Italian Franco Scapini. Who is Franco Scapini ? He's a former Formula 3000 participant and test driver for the LIFE Formula One team. John Jones, who last competed in the series in 1989, brings along Labbatt's beer as his chief sponsor.

The team consists of 16 employees, headed by team manager Andreas Leberle, who is also the chief mechanic for John Jones. Mike Albrecht is the chief on Scapini's car. Both Leberle and Albrecht are former Dick Simon employees.

The team's owner, Antonio Ferrari, is the grand-nephew of the late Enzo Ferrari. This means that Antonio's grandfather and Enzo Ferrari were brothers. The Ferrari name recognition does not necessarily please Antonio. " I do not like this publicity. Everybody writes something about it, but I was born from my father's side of the family. The other side has done nothing for me. I'm not really happy about the publicity."

Ferrari (age 35) came to America and established his team in 1988. " I owned a Group C team in Europe and I decided to sell the team and come over to the Indy cars. It was a big business opportunity to come over here. I liked it, so I stayed here." Antonio also has a degree in mechanical engineering. He, along with Alain Clarinval handle the engineering set up of both cars. The team utilizes the standard 1991 Lola chassis with Cosworth DFS power. The team rotates a total of eight engines.

Euromotorsports moved into this larger shop in March, 1991.

UNO / Shierson Racing

UNO / Shierson Racing is based in Adrian, Michigan. Team owner Bob Tezak became partners with Doug Sheirson in Mid 1990, with Tezak purchasing the remaining share at the end of the season. The team returns with MacKenzie Financial as its primary sponsor with fellow Canadian Scott Goodyear handling the driving.

Team manager Neil Micklewright is a former chief mechanic. There are several former mechanics that have moved up to the role of team manager in Indy car racing. With a mechanics backround, Micklewright was taught to oversee all of the different aspects of the team. " You get a one sided view of things as a mechanic, because your sole purpose is to get the race car put together and make sure that it's reliable. It's easy to sometimes forget the logistics that go into making things happen. I think that moving up into a managerial position, I have the same responsibilities in making sure that the cars are completed on time, etc. Then I have the added burden or concern for the budgetary constraints. You realize that you need a new part here or there, but they just don't appear out of nowhere. You have to not only make sure that it's ordered, but also that you 're able to pay for things that you 've ordered. But then you suddenly get into a position where you 've got to be on the fence, you still have to be in the position to understand the needs and the concerns of the workforce, and at the same time understand the needs and concerns of the business."

UNO / Shierson Racing, like many other medium or small teams, might have a slim chance of competing with the upper echelon teams that have Chevrolet engines. You may wonder how some of these medium efforts measure success ？ " Really, I think that we measure success in the same way that everybody else does. We go out there with the intention of winning. We wouldn't go to the race unless we felt that we could win. Being realistic, we know that sometimes the odds are stacked against us somewhat more than they would be with some other teams. Essentially, we like to come away from a race weekend and think, okay, we took everything that was there for us to take. If we can come back and say that, then we feel that we had a fairly successful weekend. That does not, and never will make up for not winning, but if we go out there and we're only quick enough that we can finish sixth, well then if we can finish sixth, and at least finish, then we feel that we've vindicated ourselves to some degree. But that doesn't make up for not winning ."
UNO / Shierson employs 18 people and utilizes a 1991 Lola/Judd combination. The team owns 10 Judd engines which are maintained by TruePower in Hilliard, Ohio. Doug Shierson remains as a consultant for the team.

Arciero Racing

Arciero Racing is owned by California construction and wine entreprenuer Frank Arciero. With all of his other business interests, Arciero relies on team manager Dennis McCormick to make most of the key decisions for the team. Dennis has been with Arciero since 1985. McCormick, who is a former mechanic, is also responsible for the daily running of the team. " You learn leadership. A team manager title today is basically what a chief mechanic was 10 or 15 years ago. The teams are growing so big, and there's so much to do, it just added another position to the team. I still have all of the responsibilities I did when I was a chief mechanic, except now I do everything from working on the race car to organizing the travel, to setting up the car, everything. It's a challenge, it's a lot of work."

David Breidenbach is the official chief mechanic for the team. Breidenbach is in his third year with the team. Rookie driver Mark Dismore was the team's choice for 1991. Working with a rookie driver is another challenge for McCormick. " It's a lot of work teaching a rookie what you 've learned over the years with different drivers. If the driver has a lot of potential, it makes it quite easy. Basically, you try to nurture him through the test miles, especially at Indianapolis. You have to teach him to have patience, not to rush into things, and everything will come to him eventually ."

Although Frank Arciero does not frequent the race shop in Indianapolis, he remains in close contact with McCormick. " I talk to him by telephone all the time, once or twice a day. He knows everything that's going on ."

Chip Ganassi Racing

Chip Ganassi and Eddie Cheever are in their second year together. Ganassi, who has driven in five Indianapolis 500 mile races from 1982 to 1986, has found that being a former driver has a great advantage with working with Eddie Cheever. " It's fairly easy because he and I have sort of an understanding of each other. It's sort of an unspoken understanding that we don't have to verbalize everything to communicate. I look at it more or less as a coach to a player kind of thing. It's more of a motivation type of thing, a perspective."

Chip retired from driving and eased into a partnership with Pat Patrick in 1989. The two split a year later with Ganassi taking the shop and the Chevy engines. You might wonder if Chip ever gets the urge to drive an Indy car again ？ " I don't have the urge to go out and do it competitively anymore. Besides, I can't fit in the cars anymore (laughing). Eddie had this special seat made specifically for him, I can't hardly get my knees to fit past the bulkhead, under the steering wheel."

A lot of people may wonder why a former driver, who is only 33 years old, decided to buy a team ? " I think that it was just an obvious love for the sport. I think that I have a lot to give to the sport, and since I can't give it as a driver, I don't feel like being a corner worker, so there's nothing left but being a car owner. I'm not a very good mechanic so I wouldn't do well at that."

Team manager Tom Anderson oversees a total of 32 employees. Chris Griffis returns as chief mechanic with Ken Anderson serving as the team engineer. Ken is a former Penske and Ligier Formula One engineer.

Ganassi purchased three 1991 Lolas, and has 14 Chevrolet engines. Target, along with Scotch and several of its smaller co-op sponsors support the effort.

A.J. Foyt Enterprises

In 1990, A.J. Foyt hired veteran crew chief and team manager Phil Casey to turn his team around. The team had gained Chevrolet power, and was starting to put in some decent finishes when A.J. had his devastating crash at Elkhart Lake in September of 1990.

When Foyt hired Casey to manage his team, observers around the sport felt that Foyt had finally hired the right person to help him be competitive again. Phil has worked in the sport since the 1960's, and is truly one of the last of the old style mechanics that are still active.

Race fans often see two sides of A.J. Foyt. There's the more composed and personable side, and there's the dreaded bear and ornery side. Working for A.J. was always thought to be far less than easy. However, Casey decribes working for the first four-time Indy 500 winner as being no problem: " We 've always gotten along really well, we haven't had any problems. He's got a lot of knowledge, and he likes to try diffferent things. He's raced a long time so if he wants to try something new, he tries it." Indeed, acquaintances remark that Phil is probably in the most easy going mood in years. To add a little insight, Phil is normally the type of person who thinks and works at 200 miles per hour.

With Foyt being so busy with other business interests, maintaining a normal work schedule can be sometimes difficult, but always works out. " It hasn't really been that much of a problem. He'll call on the phone to tell us what he wants done. If he's in town he'll come by the shop and spend some time. If he's on the road, and he wants to try something different, he'll call us and tell us what to do."

Longtime employee Jack Starnes still works for the team as the shop foreman and parts fabricator. Craig Baranouski serves as the chief mechanic. Foyt purchased two 1991 Lola for what is suppose to be his final season before becoming a full-time car owner.

The team rotates a total of seven Chevrolet engines.

Coming from the old school of the 1960's, Casey admits that hes lost some of his spirit in working in this modern era of racing. " It's not quite as much fun because back then you tried a lot of different things. Now everything is on computers and down to engineering. Most of the teams that are sucessful now have two or three engineers. We used to build our own cars and we'd go racing. It's a lot different now where you just buy everything. It's progress. It's like anything else, you go along with the times. Everything keeps progressing and changing more and more. I think that it will eventually become more like Formula One racing."

Casey, along with Foyt handle their own set up engineering. " A.J. comes in and tells us what he wants to do, then we talk about it and if it works well, than we stick with it at the next race. He knows what he wants."

A.J. Foyt Enterpises employs seven full-time people with additional weekend support at the race track. The team is based in Houston, Texas.

Winkelmann Racing

Roy Winkelmann has fulfilled a dream he's been working on for many years with the formation of his own Indy car team. The racing fraternity applauded Winkelmann for hiring talented driver John Paul Jr. to drive his 1991 Lola Cosworth. " John Paul Jr. was my first choice based on his record." Winkelmann states. Indeed, John Paul Jr. won the 1983 Michigan 500 while only making his fourth Indy car start.

" I have been working on this deal for many years," says Winkelmann. "I nearly had a deal put together about five years ago with Al Unser Jr., Coors and Lotus, but it didn't all work out and I was forced to abandon the project only a few months before the start of the season. Lotus had built a more advanced carbon-fiber chassis that would not meet the CART technical requirements at the time. The car does exist, but it sits in a museum today."

Winkelmann's primary sponsor, SYNPETCO, is a manufacurer of rocket propulsion systems. Their parent corporation CEROS Aerospace is the teams associate sponsor. Both of these companies are in the private aerospace business. " With the increasing need to put commercial satellite systems into the Earth's orbit, the opportunities for the private aerospace sector are wide open", said Winkelmann. " To achieve marketing visability through Indy car racing will give our sponsors the awareness and exposure that they require." Winkelmann Racing is based in Indianapolis. Former Kraco team manager 'Haff' Haffendon serves as team manager.

Basic Race Car Dimensions

Drawing by J. Kirk Russell (Courtesy of C.A.R.T.)

56

March 17 Gold Coast Indy Car Grand Prix

PACIFIC OCEAN
N
MAIN BEACH PARADE
CABLE ST
PACIFIC STREET
PONTOON BRIDGE
NERANG RIVER
START/FINISH
PIT AREA
MACINTOSH ISLAND
SERISIER AVE
HILL PARADE
COMMODORE DRIVE
ADMIRALTY DRIVE
FERNY AVENUE
HIGMAN ST
MAIN BEACH PDE
VIEW AVENUE
OCEAN AVE
PANDANUS AVE
STAGHORN AVENUE
PALM AVENUE
CYPRESS AVENUE
BIRT AVENUE
NORFOLK AVENUE
PINE AVENUE

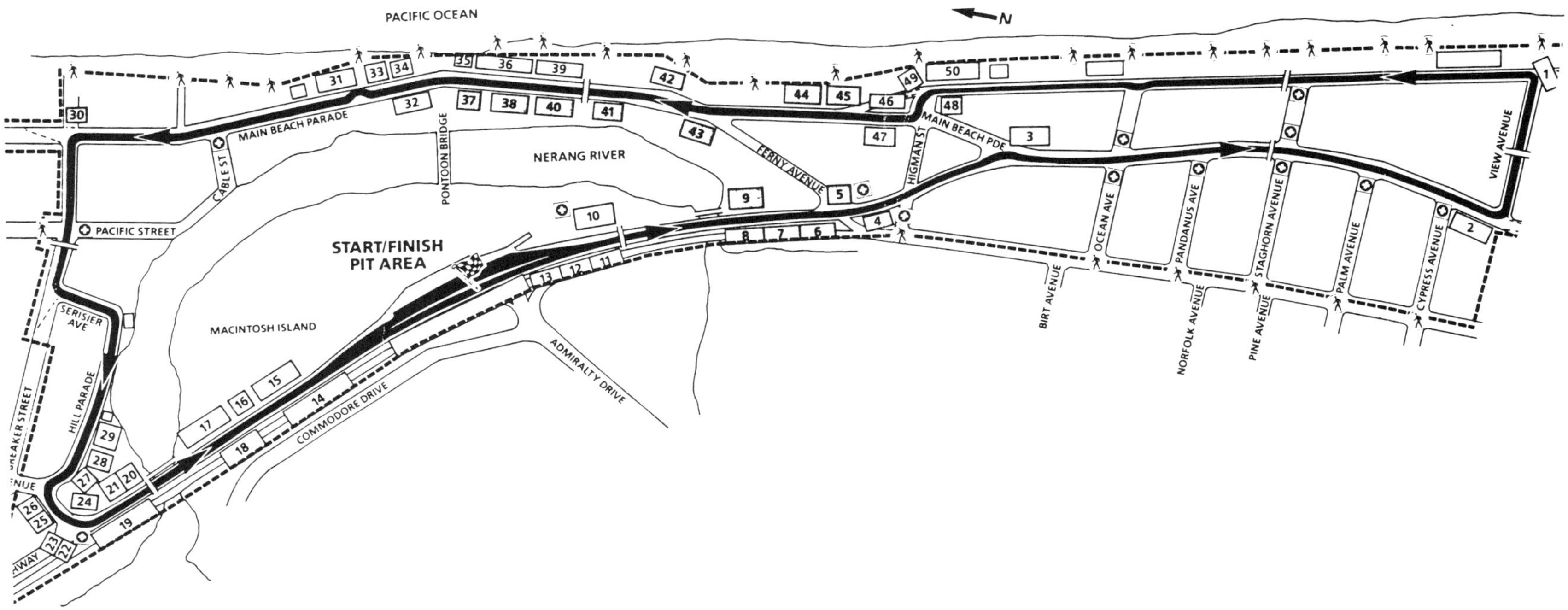

2.793 Mile Road Course (Ticket Information 61-75-316999)

1.67 Mile Temporary Road Course (Ticket Information 213-436-9953)

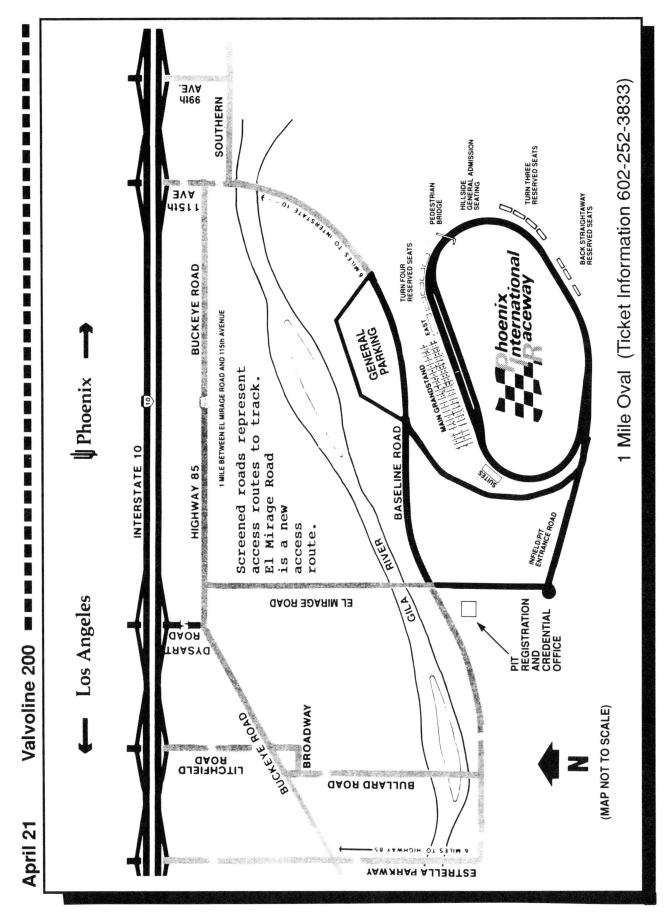

April 21   Valvoline 200

← Los Angeles   Phoenix →

Phoenix International Raceway

1 Mile Oval (Ticket Information 602-252-3833)

(MAP NOT TO SCALE)

N

INTERSTATE 10

HIGHWAY 85

BUCKEYE ROAD

SOUTHERN

99th AVE.

115th AVE.

Screened roads represent access routes to track. El Mirage Road is a new access route.

1 MILE BETWEEN EL MIRAGE ROAD AND 115th AVENUE

6 MILES TO INTERSTATE 10

EL MIRAGE ROAD

DYSART ROAD

LITCHFIELD ROAD

BUCKEYE ROAD

BROADWAY

BULLARD ROAD

ESTRELLA PARKWAY

6 MILES TO HIGHWAY 85

GILA RIVER

BASELINE ROAD

GENERAL PARKING

PIT REGISTRATION AND CREDENTIAL OFFICE

INFIELD/PIT ENTRANCE ROAD

MAIN GRANDSTAND

EAST

SUITES

TURN FOUR RESERVED SEATS

PEDESTRIAN BRIDGE

HILLSIDE GENERAL ADMISSION SEATING

TURN THREE RESERVED SEATS

BACK STRAIGHTAWAY RESERVED SEATS

59

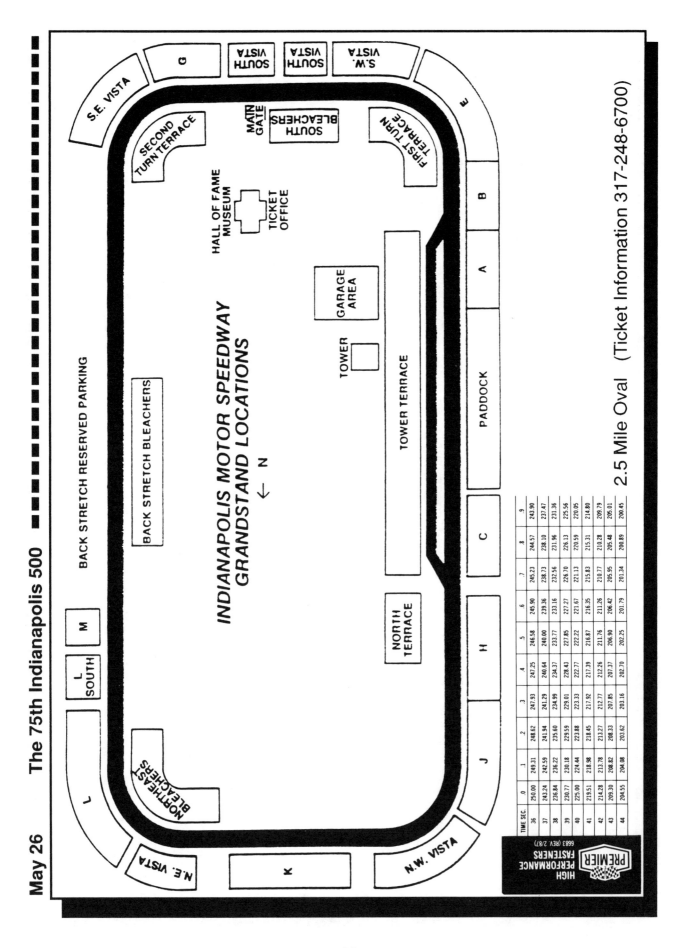

INDIANAPOLIS MOTOR SPEEDWAY GRANDSTAND LOCATIONS

2.5 Mile Oval   (Ticket Information 317-248-6700)

TIME SEC.	0	1	2	3	4	5	6	7	8	9
36	250.00	249.31	248.62	247.93	247.25	246.58	245.90	245.23	244.57	243.90
37	243.24	242.59	241.94	241.29	240.64	240.00	239.36	238.73	238.10	237.47
38	236.84	236.22	235.60	234.99	234.37	233.77	233.16	232.56	231.96	231.36
39	230.77	230.18	229.59	229.01	228.43	227.85	227.27	226.70	226.13	225.56
40	225.00	224.44	223.88	223.33	222.77	222.22	221.67	221.13	220.59	220.05
41	219.51	218.98	218.45	217.92	217.39	216.87	216.35	215.83	215.31	214.80
42	214.28	213.78	213.27	212.77	212.26	211.76	211.26	210.77	210.28	209.79
43	209.30	208.82	208.33	207.85	207.37	206.90	206.42	205.95	205.48	205.01
44	204.55	204.08	203.62	203.16	202.70	202.25	201.79	201.34	200.89	200.45

PREMIER HIGH PERFORMANCE FASTENERS
6683 (REV. 2/87)

June 2   Miller Genuine Draft 200 ■■■■■■■■■■■■■■■■■

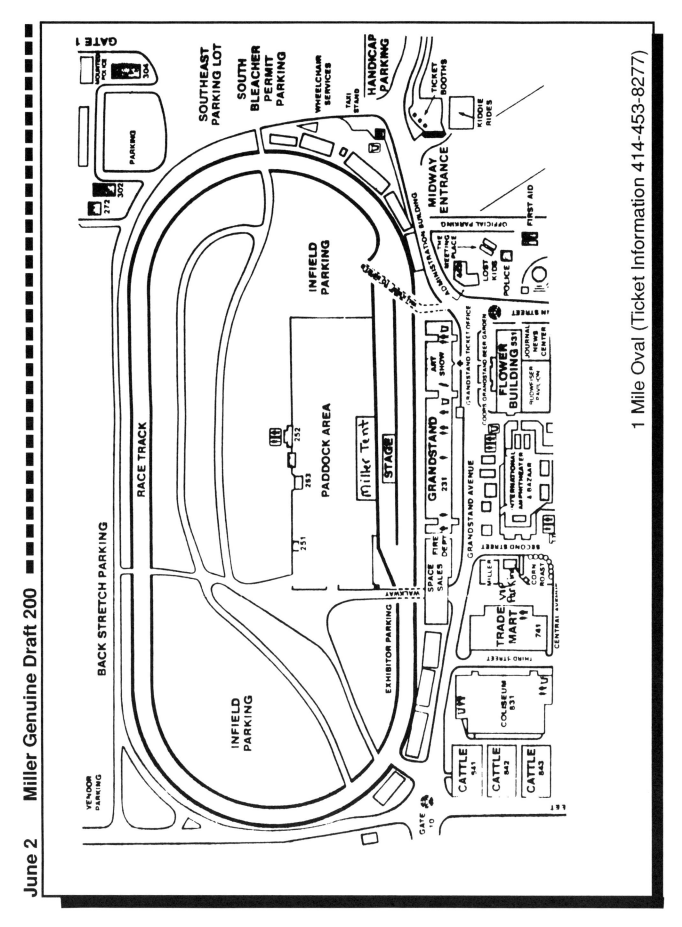

1 Mile Oval (Ticket Information 414-453-8277)

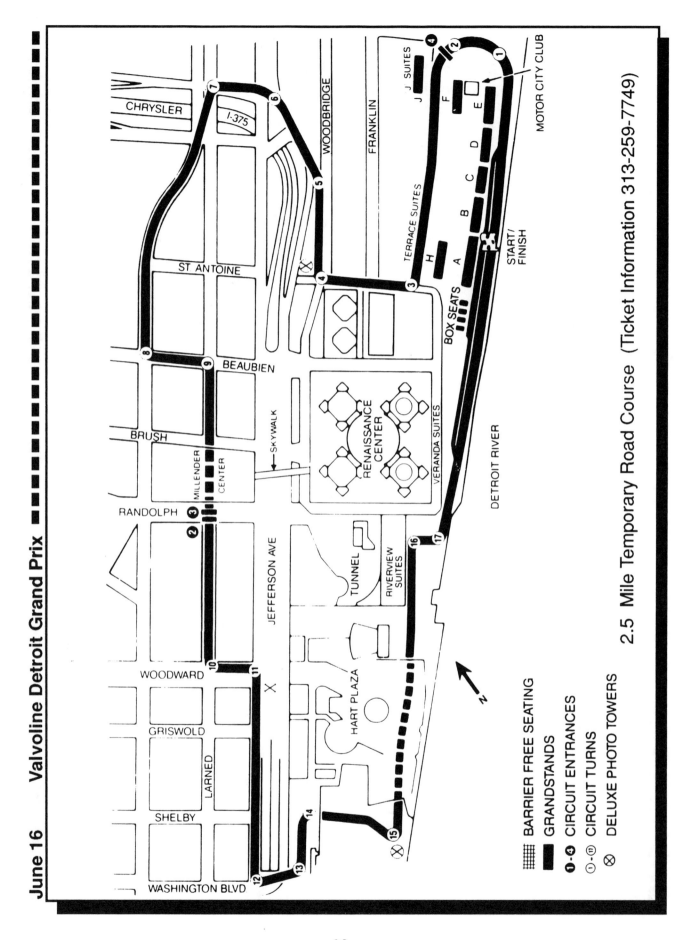

June 16   Valvoline Detroit Grand Prix

2.5 Mile Temporary Road Course (Ticket Information 313-259-7749)

BARRIER FREE SEATING
GRANDSTANDS
❶-❹ CIRCUIT ENTRANCES
①-⑪ CIRCUIT TURNS
⊗ DELUXE PHOTO TOWERS

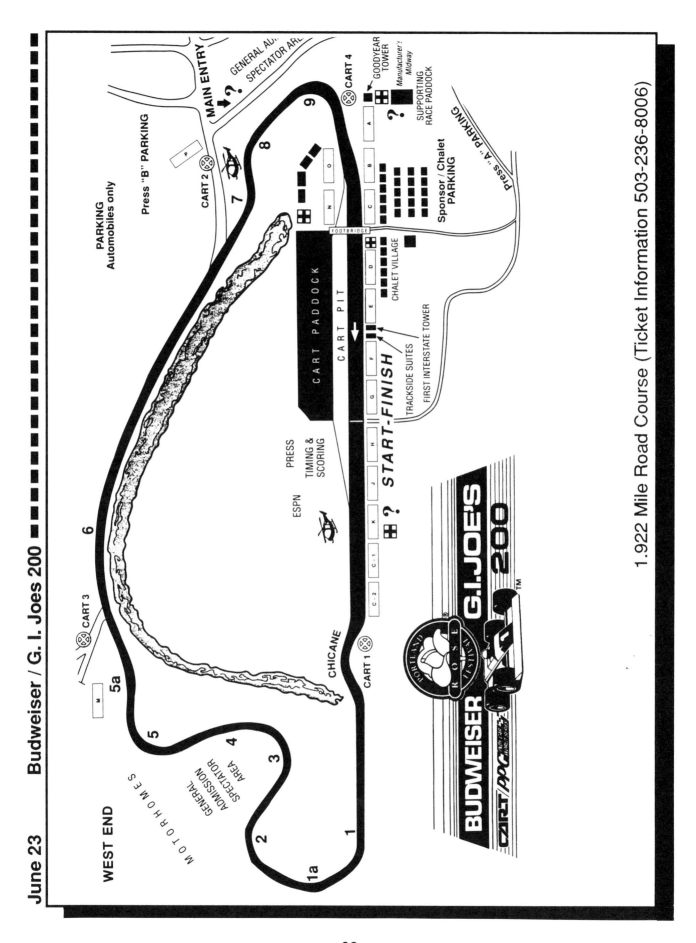

June 23   Budweiser / G. I. Joes 200

WEST END

1.922 Mile Road Course (Ticket Information 503-236-8006)

63

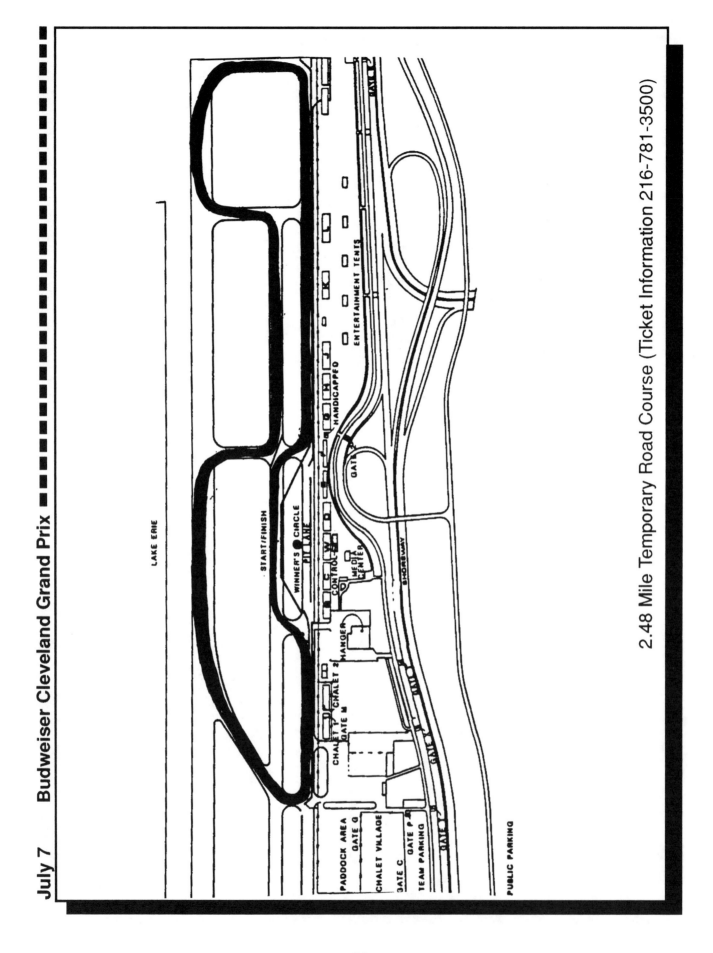

July 7   Budweiser Cleveland Grand Prix

2.48 Mile Temporary Road Course (Ticket Information 216-781-3500)

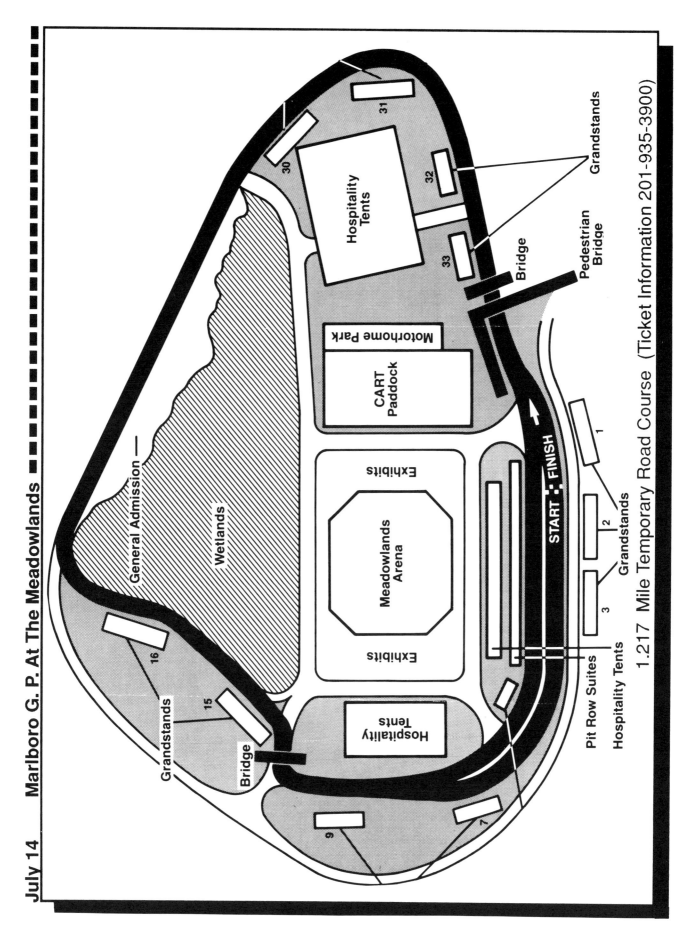

July 14 **Marlboro G. P. At The Meadowlands**

Hospitality Tents

Grandstands

Grandstands

Bridge

Pedestrian Bridge

31

30

32

33

Motorhome Park

CART Paddock

General Admission —

Wetlands

Exhibits

Meadowlands Arena

Exhibits

START · FINISH

Grandstands

1

2

3

Pit Row Suites

Hospitality Tents

Hospitality Tents

Grandstands

Bridge

15

16

9

7

1.217 Mile Temporary Road Course (Ticket Information 201-935-3900)

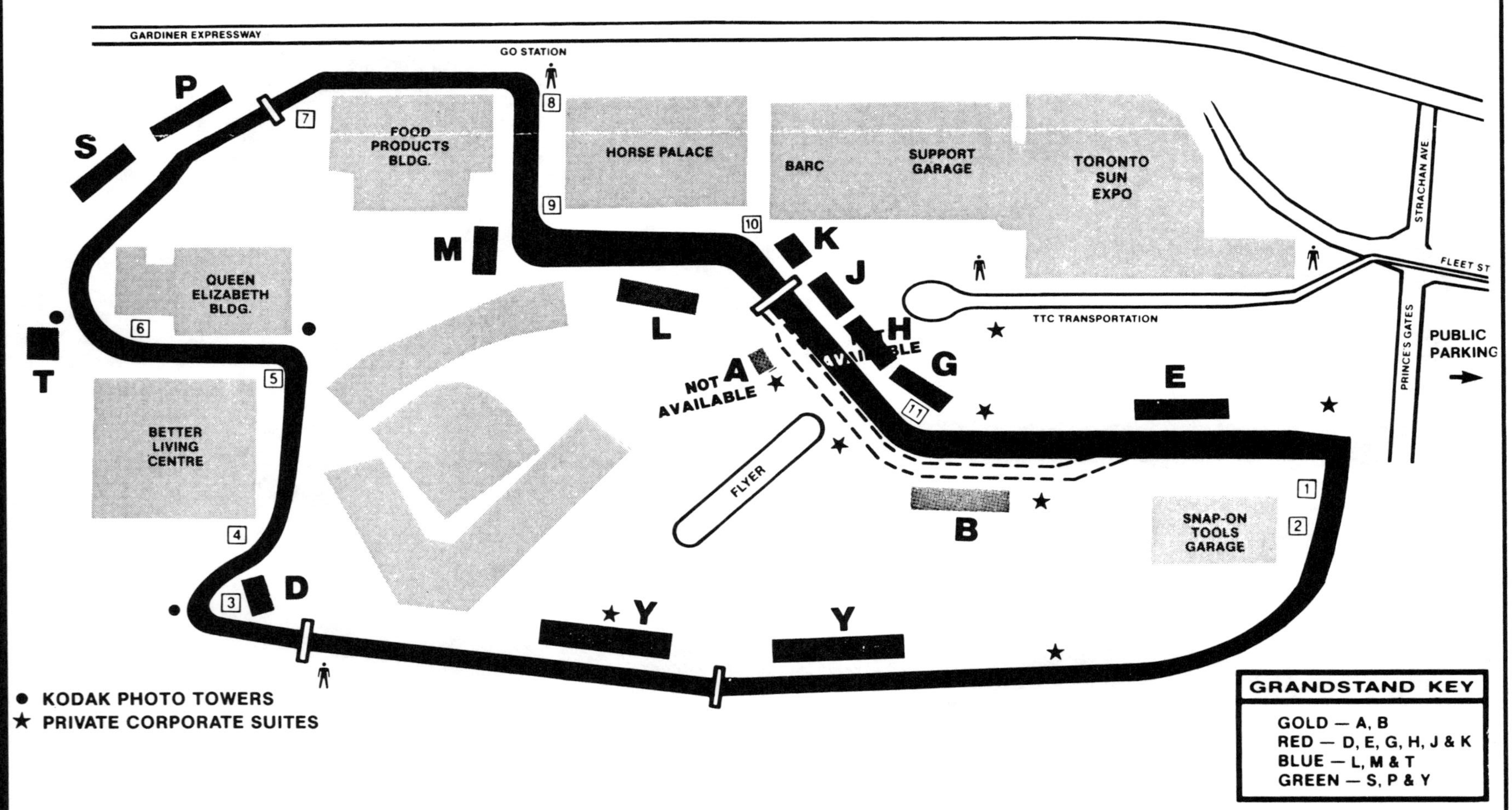

Molson Indy Toronto

July 21

1.76 Mile Road Course (Ticket Information 416-595-5445)

GRANDSTAND KEY

GOLD — A, B
RED — D, E, G, H, J & K
BLUE — L, M & T
GREEN — S, P & Y

- KODAK PHOTO TOWERS
★ PRIVATE CORPORATE SUITES

FLEET ST
STRACHAN AVE
PUBLIC PARKING
PRINCE'S GATES

TORONTO SUN EXPO
TTC TRANSPORTATION
SUPPORT GARAGE
BARC
HORSE PALACE
FOOD PRODUCTS BLDG.
GO STATION
GARDINER EXPRESSWAY
QUEEN ELIZABETH BLDG.
BETTER LIVING CENTRE
SNAP-ON TOOLS GARAGE
FLYER

NOT AVAILABLE

A B D E G H J K L M P S T Y

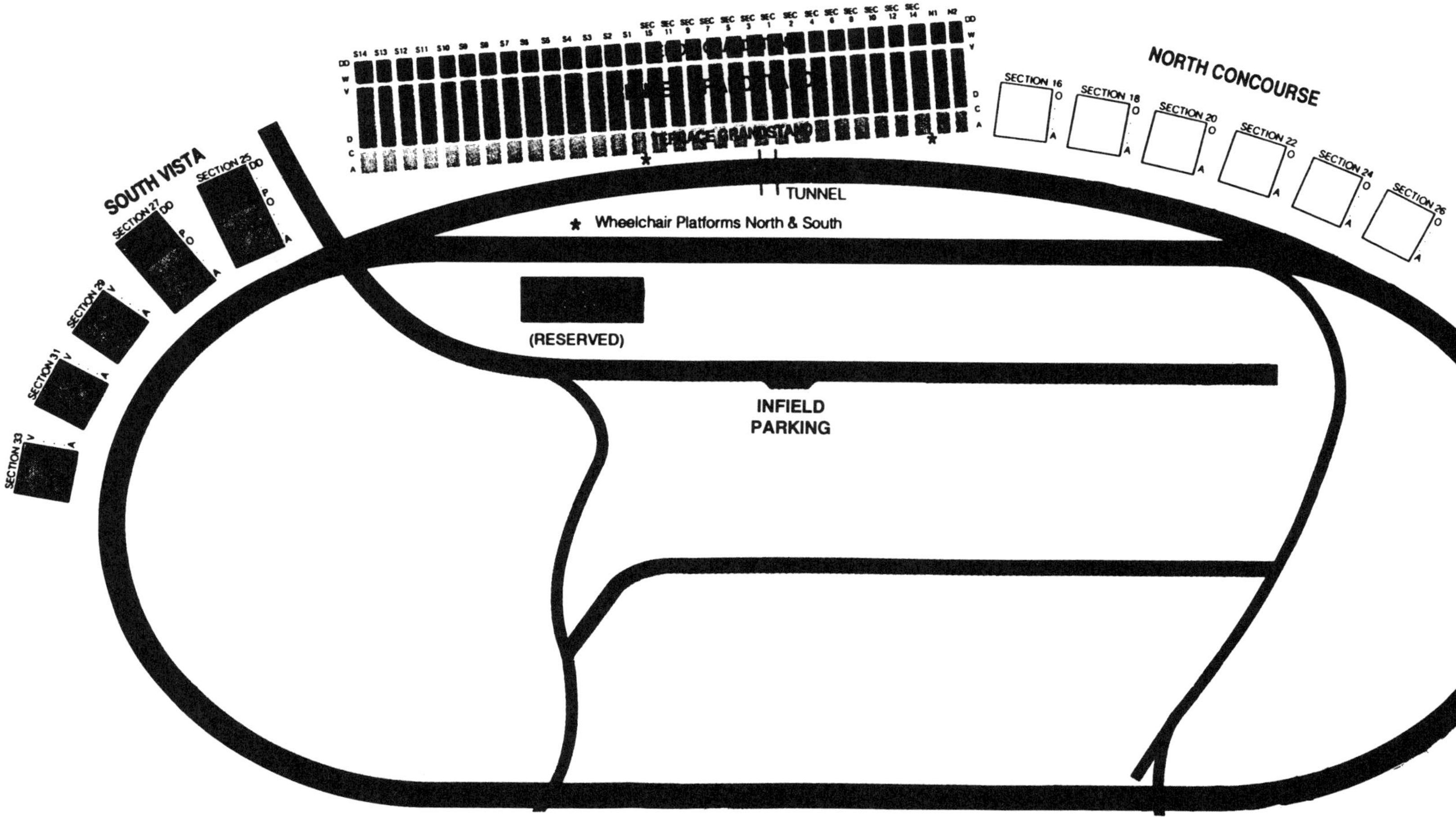

August 4   Marlboro 500

NORTH CONCOURSE

SECTION 16
SECTION 18
SECTION 20
SECTION 22
SECTION 24
SECTION 26

TUNNEL

★ Wheelchair Platforms North & South

(RESERVED)

INFIELD PARKING

SOUTH VISTA

SECTION 29
SECTION 27
SECTION 29
SECTION 31
SECTION 33

2 Mile Oval (Ticket Information 517-592-6671)

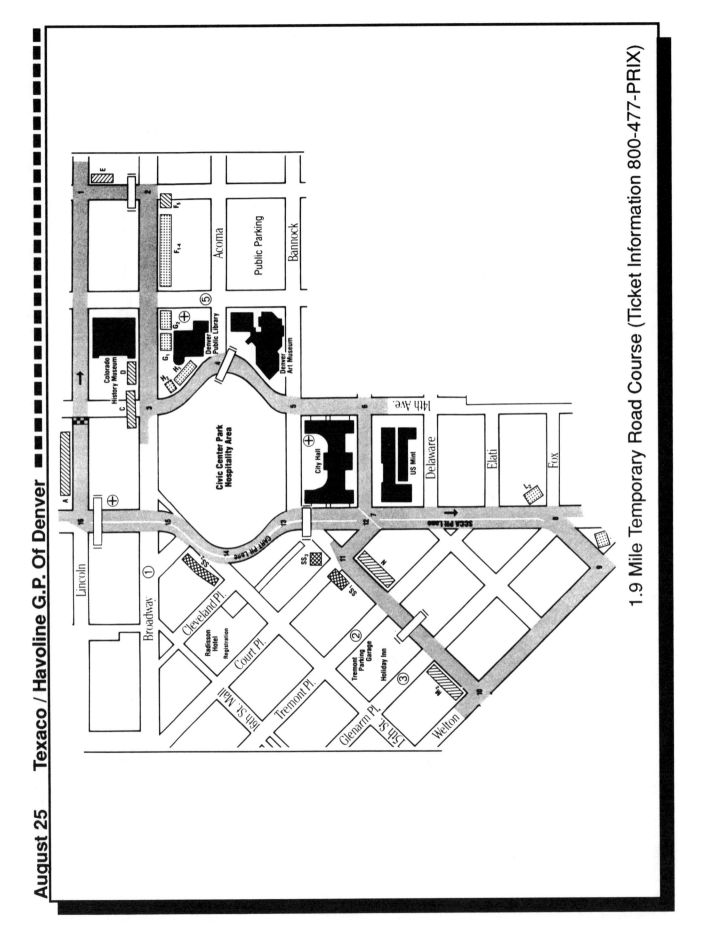

August 25   Texaco / Havoline G.P. Of Denver

1.9 Mile Temporary Road Course (Ticket Information 800-477-PRIX)

1.704 Mile Temporary Road Course (Ticket Information 604-280-INDY)

Mid Ohio
SPORTS CAR COURSE
LEXINGTON, OHIO

2.4 Mile Road Course (Ticket Information 800-MID-OHIO)

N

Q

O

R

N

V

L

K

M

Q

K

R

Q

T

Q

S

T

I

X

H

J

VC

G   F

F   F   R   E

F

POND

Q

W

U

Q

Z

Q

T

D

Q

T

C

A

B

◄ COLUMBUS/314

STEAM CORNERS ROAD

LEGEND

A	MID-OHIO REGISTRATION	N	BUDWEISER WALK-OVER BRIDGE
B	MID-OHIO MAIN OFFICE	O	NISSAN WALK-OVER BRIDGE
C	CAMEL ENTRANCE GATE (SOUTH)	P	NORTH ENTRANCE GATE
D	MAINTENANCE BLDG.	Q	CONCESSION STANDS
E	GOODYEAR TOWER	R	RESTROOMS
F	GARAGES	S	UNDERGROUND WALKWAY
G	HORTON MEDICAL BLDG.	T	OBSERVATION MOUNDS
H	NISSAN COMMUNICATIONS BLDG.	U	MAC TOOL TECH BLDG
I	ELECTRONIC SCORETOWER	V	COMMUNICATION TOWER
J	GOODYEAR DRIVE-OVER BRIDGE	W	PICNIC SHELTER
K	GRANDSTANDS 1 & 2	X	CHAMPIONSHIP ROW
L	CAMEL OBSERVATION DECK	Z	FUEL FACILITY
M	MANUFACTURERS MIDWAY	VC	VICTORY CIRCLE

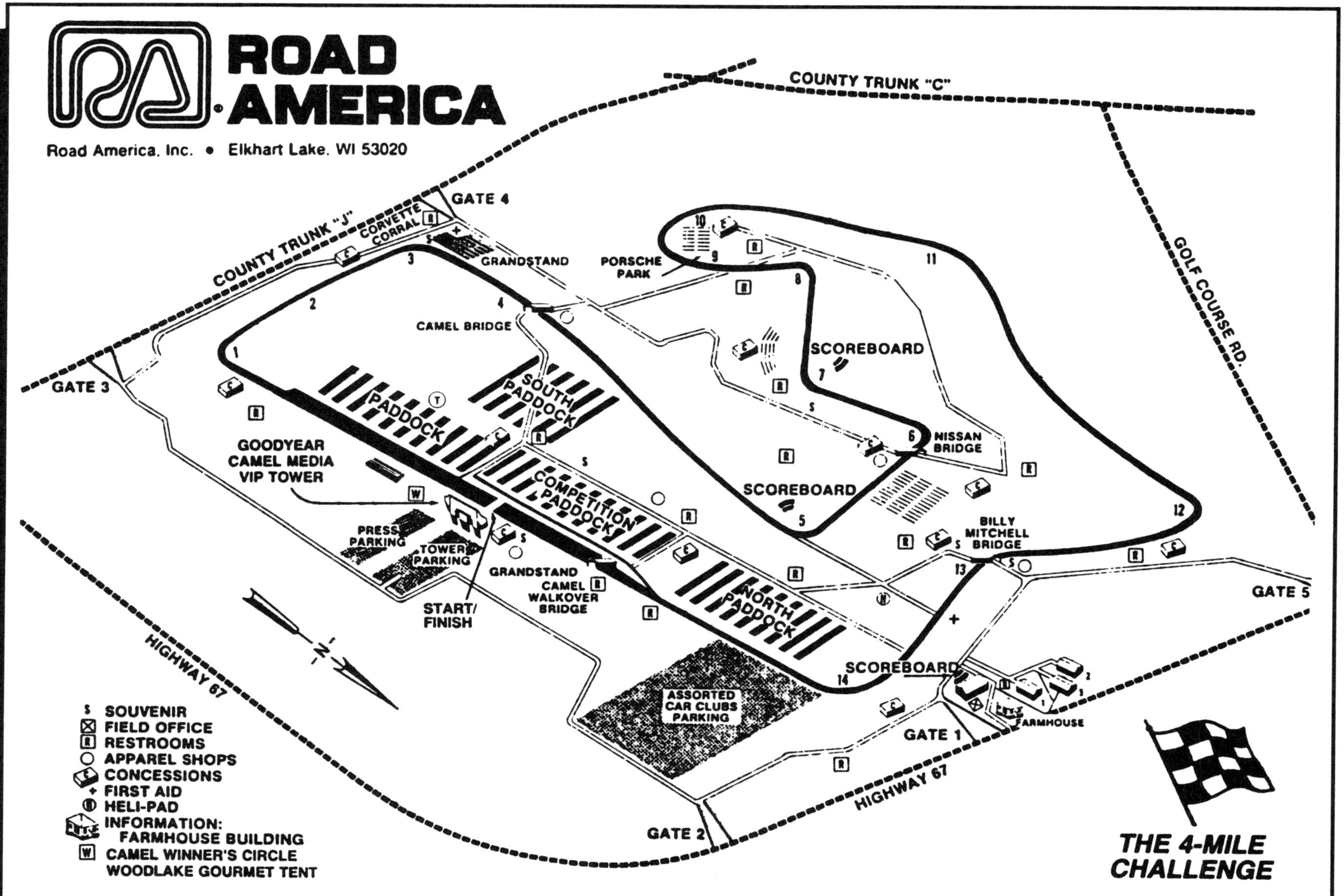

September 22   Texaco / Havoline 200

ROAD AMERICA

Road America, Inc. • Elkhart Lake, WI 53020

THE 4-MILE CHALLENGE

4 Mile Road Course (Ticket Information 800-365-RACE)

GOLF COURSE RD.

COUNTY TRUNK "C"

COUNTY TRUNK "J"

GATE 5
GATE 1
GATE 2
GATE 3
GATE 4

HIGHWAY 67
HIGHWAY 67

FARMHOUSE

ASSORTED CAR CLUBS PARKING

SCOREBOARD
SCOREBOARD
SCOREBOARD
SCOREBOARD

NISSAN BRIDGE
BILLY MITCHELL BRIDGE
CAMEL BRIDGE
CAMEL WALKOVER BRIDGE

PORSCHE PARK

SOUTH PADDOCK
NORTH PADDOCK
COMPETITION PADDOCK
PADDOCK

CORVETTE CORRAL

GRANDSTAND
GRANDSTAND

START/ FINISH

TOWER PARKING
PRESS PARKING

GOODYEAR CAMEL MEDIA VIP TOWER

12 11 13 14 6 7 8 9 10 5 4 3 2 1

$ SOUVENIR
⊠ FIELD OFFICE
♿ RESTROOMS
○ APPAREL SHOPS
    CONCESSIONS
+ FIRST AID
⊕ HELI-PAD
INFORMATION:
    FARMHOUSE BUILDING
W CAMEL WINNER'S CIRCLE
    WOODLAKE GOURMET TENT

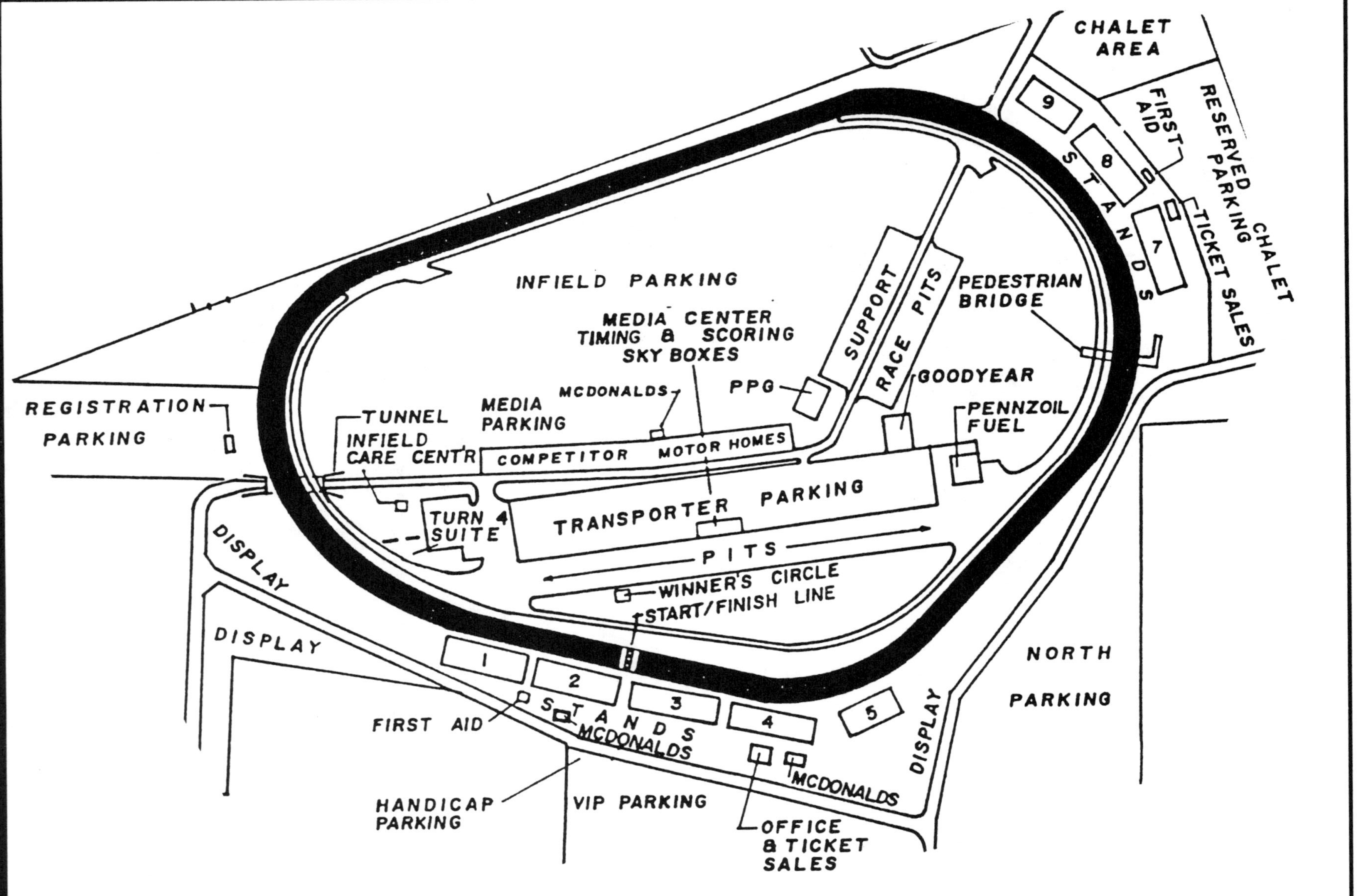

October 6 ■ Bosch Spark Plug Grand Prix ■

RESERVED CHALET PARKING

TICKET SALES

CHALET AREA

FIRST AID

9   8   7

S T A N D S

PEDESTRIAN BRIDGE

GOODYEAR

PENNZOIL FUEL

NORTH PARKING

DISPLAY

5

MCDONALDS

OFFICE & TICKET SALES

RACE PITS

SUPPORT

PPG

MOTOR HOMES

TRANSPORTER PARKING

TRANSPORTER

PITS

WINNER'S CIRCLE

START/FINISH LINE

4

MCDONALDS

INFIELD PARKING

MEDIA CENTER TIMING & SCORING SKY BOXES

MCDONALDS

MEDIA PARKING

COMPETITOR PARKING

TURN 4 SUITE

3

2

S T A N D S

MCDONALDS

VIP PARKING

TUNNEL

INFIELD CARE CENTER

1

FIRST AID

HANDICAP PARKING

REGISTRATION PARKING

DISPLAY

DISPLAY

1 Mile Oval (Ticket Information 215-759-8000)

72

2.214 Mile Road Course (Ticket Information 408-648-5100)

The 1991 Lola T9100 (drawing by Tony Matthews)

Acknowledgments

Michael Andretti
Bruce Ashmore
Tony Bettenhausen
Dr. Henry Bock
Andrew Broadley
Lon Bromely
Phil Casey
Dale Coyne
Ron Dawes
Danny Drinan
Wayne Eaton
Antonio Ferarri
Galen Fox
Chip Ganassi

Walter Gerber
Kent Gerhardt
Barry Green
Jim Hall II
Paul Harcus
Lee Kunzman
Tim Lombardi
Dennis McCormick
Jim McGee
Neil Mickelwright
John Miller
Rick Mears
Kyle Moyer

Ed Nathman
Tony Phelps
Scott Pruett
Geri Schneider
Dick Simon
Dan Taylor
Tony Van Dongen
Bill Vukovich II
Steve Weaver
Doug Wendt
Trev Weston
Jim Wright
Mary Ellen Wright

The Indianapolis 500 Yearbook, by Carl Hungness, 1980-1990

C.A.R.T. Media Guide

Edited by Jill Taylor

About The Author

Rick Amabile is the grandson of the legendary two-time Indianapolis 500 winner Bill Vukovich. Born in Fresno, California, Rick has been addicted to Indy car racing since the age of 13. He began working in Indy car racing part-time for Team VDS, while still a junior in high school.

Later, he went on to work with various teams including the winning Kraco team in 1986, before going on to pursue other interests. Rick stays close to racing by working for Premier Industrial Corp. at its Gasoline Alley service room each year during the month of May. Rick is also the author of *Inside Indy Car Racing-1990* and *The Insider's Guide to Indy Car Racing*. *Inside Indy Car Racing* is an annual edition with different features each year.

INDY CAR FANS

NEED A GIFT IDEA?

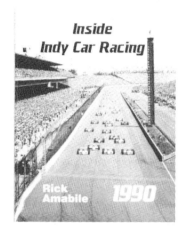

This exciting book will take you to the inner elements of Indy Car racing. Have you ever wondered how much money it takes to sponsor or operate a team? Are you curious about how much drivers and crewmembers really earn?   Former crewmember, Rick Amabile, details every facet from cars and drivers, to the history of various subjects that comprise this fast growing sport.

Sections include: Cars: Lola, Penske, Porsche/March, Alfa Romeo, Lola black box system, Chevrolet system, Porsche telemetry, tires, Aerodynamics, Why England?, Formula 1 to Indy Car comparison. Engines: Chevy Indy V-8, Cosworth, Buick, Porsche, Alfa Romeo, Judd, Engine maintenance, Turbocharging, Fuel, Engine oil. Crewmembers: Routine, Designers-Engineers, Mechanics, Team Managers, Respective salary ranges.   Drivers: The process of "Buying a ride", Driver income, Unifoms and helmet information, driver statistics chart. The history of the Indy 500: Track surface, Purse, Garage area, Time trials, Past winners, Statistics and trivia. Team Backrounds: Penske, Patrick, Galles/Kraco, Ganassi, Porsche, Newman/Haas, Truesports. Shierson/O'Donnell, A.J. Foyt, Raynor/Cosby, Dick Simon, Vince Granatelli, Arciero, Leader Cards, Team Budgets, Transporter cost information. Sponsors and Marketing: How much does it cost to sponsor a team?, Event sponsorships, Contingency sponsors, Audience analysis, Television coverage, Adding up television exposure, In-car camera details. Race Tracks: Course diagrams with the history of each event. Safety: Car safety factors, Car construction, CART medical team, Accident survey, Fire prevention. The history of CART and USAC: Buying into CART, The end of the Frasco era, Rookie driver test, Points, Past champions, AAA/USAC Past champions. Glossar and Contributions to the auto industry.

The Author has rejected the traditional, often sugary approach to writing about Indy Car racing. Amabile gets down to business and uncovers the behind the scenes details and otherwise untold secrets. This fascinating book is guaranteed to satisfy any Indy Car enthusiast.

" An intersting 62 page book that lets the reader in on such things as salaries of drivers and crewmen, legal battles and other items not usually found in public prints."
Chris Economaki,
National Speed Sport News

"It's a good book and contains a lot of material."
Roger Penske

8 1/2 x 11   62 Pages, 15 Illustrations ## $ 11.95

Please send check or money order to:

P.O. Box 25156 • Fresno, CA 93729

Please include $3.00 for postage & handling
Please allow 2 to 3 weeks for delivery

SATISFACTION GUARANTEED
 If for any reason you are not satisfied
with your purchase, you may return
it for a full refund.

1990 PPG INDY CAR WORLD SERIES DRIVERS PERFORMANCE CHART
FOLLOWING FINAL 1990 EVENT

RANK	DRIVER	PTS	STS	RUN AT FIN	TOP FIN	TMS LED	LAPS LED (2040)	LAPS COMP (2040)	MILES COMP (3567.337)	PURSE
1	AL UNSER, Jr.	210	16	13	1	19	449	1853	3261.161	$1,936,833
2	MICHAEL ANDRETTI	181	16	11	1	15	512	1655	2916.121	$1,303,526
3	RICK MEARS	168	16	14	1	3	136	1979	3443.570	$1,414,744
4	BOBBY RAHAL	153	16	14	2	11	222	1867	3320.704	$1,462,458
5	EMERSON FITTIPALDI	144	16	13	1	10	412	1880	3259.634	$1,513,176
6	DANNY SULLIVAN	139	16	10	1	9	163	1495	2494.707	$965,161
7	MARIO ANDRETTI	136	16	11	2	8	69	1515	2635.356	$976,721
8	ARIE LUYENDYK	90	16	11	1	5	50	1584	2897.830	$1,747,984
9	EDDIE CHEEVER	80	16	11	3	0	0	1808	3182.450	$869,720
10	JOHN ANDRETTI	51	16	8	5	0	0	1563	2722.013	$456,594
11	A.J. FOYT, Jr.	42	14	10	5	0	0	1403	2620.852	$578,744
12	RAUL BOESEL	42	16	10	6	0	0	1504	2565.489	$579,913
13	SCOTT GOODYEAR	36	16	12	7	0	0	1766	3069.881	$429,724
14	TEO FABI	33	16	8	3	2	27	1381	2336.946	$614,335
15	SCOTT BRAYTON	28	16	10	7	0	0	1528	2667.624	$592,442
16	ROBERTO GUERRERO	24	15	5	5	0	0	1371	2400.354	$471,375
17	MIKE GROFF	17	12	7	7	0	0	1029	1964.982	$257,628
18	DIDIER THEYS	15	12	7	7	0	0	956	1817.747	$452,218
19	DOMINIC DOBSON	12	11	5	8	0	0	734	1405.361	$325,390
20	PANCHO CARTER	9	9	3	8	0	0	927	1508.000	$323,967
21	JON BEEKHUIS	7	9	2	8	0	0	559	1199.460	$127,024
22	JEFF WOOD	7	10	4	10	0	0	636	1133.123	$117,269
23	KEVIN COGAN	4	2	1	9	0	0	321	737.500	$164,630
24	TONY BETTENHAUSEN	4	11	6	10	0	0	773	1357.740	$345,710
25	DEAN HALL	4	15	9	11	0	0	1277	2350.415	$444,735
26	WILLY T. RIBBS	3	8	2	10	0	0	357	660.281	$102,020
27	WALLY DALLENBACH, Jr.	2	3	1	11	0	0	158	327.662	$73,214
28	RANDY LEWIS	2	16	8	12	0	0	1231	2266.924	$448,129
29	GUIDO DACCO	1	6	4	12	0	0	565	853.112	$84,762
30	BUDDY LAZIER	1	6	2	12	0	0	435	694.298	$178,031
31	HIRO MATSUSHITA	1	10	4	12	0	0	586	1139.076	$216,160
32	MICHAEL GREENFIELD	1	7	0	12	0	0	405	615.639	$69,350
33	TERO PALMROTH	1	3	1	12	0	0	218	512.925	$164,466
34	BILLY VUKOVICH	0	2	1	13	0	0	312	675.000	$148,787
35	AL UNSER	0	1	1	13	0	0	186	465.000	$141,387
36	JIM CRAWFORD	0	2	1	15	0	0	229	503.500	$140,272
37	JOHN PAUL, Jr.	0	1	0	16	0	0	176	440.000	$150,276
38	JOSEPH SPOSATO	0	1	1	17	0	0	76	168.264	$4,250
39	JEFF ANDRETTI	0	1	0	17	0	0	117	117.000	$16,566
40	ROSS BENTLEY	0	1	1	18	0	0	77	131.208	$13,714
41	GEOFF BRABHAM	0	1	1	19	0	0	161	402.500	$131,688
42	ROCKY MORAN	0	1	0	25	0	0	88	220.000	$124,580
43	STEVE BREN	0	1	0	25	0	0	5	8.350	$11,400
44	TOM SNEVA	0	1	0	30	0	0	48	120.000	$110,338
45	GARY BETTENHAUSEN	0	1	0	31	0	0	39	97.500	$109,464
46	STAN FOX	0	1	0	33	0	0	10	25.000	$108,021
47	JOHN MORTON	0	0	0		0	0	0	0.000	$10,212
48	FULVIO BALLABIO	0	0	0		0	0	0	0.000	$11,708
49	SALT WALTHER	0	0	0		0	0	0	0.000	$0

All Statistics Concluded After The 1990 Season Final

Driver	Age	Team For 1991	First Indy Car Start	Total Starts	Poles	First Win	Total Wins	Residence
Jeff Andretti	26	Bayside	Milwaukee,1990	1	--	--	--	Nazareth, PA
John Andretti	28	Hall / VDS	Road America,1987	28	--	--	--	Indianapolis, IN
Mario Andretti	51	Newman / Haas	Trenton,1964	343	51	Hoosier GP,1965	51	Nazareth, PA
Michael Andretti	28	Newman / Haas	Las Vegas,1983	112	12	Long Beach,1986	15	Nazareth, PA
Jon Beekhuis	31	N/A	Toronto,1989	12	--	--	--	Salinas, CA
Scott Brayton	32	Dick Simon	Phoenix,1981	91	--	--	--	Coldwater, MI
Gary Bettenhausen	49	Menard	Phoenix,1966	185	2	Phoenix,1968	4	Monrovia, IN
Tony Bettenhausen	39	Bettenhausen	Texas,1979	82	--	--	--	Indianapolis, IN
Eddie Cheever	33	Chip Ganassi	Miami,1986	17	--	--	--	Rome, Italy
Kevin Cogan	35	N/A	Indianapolis,1981	112	2	Phoenix,1986	1	Palos VerdesEstates, CA
Jim Crawford	43	Bernstein	Long Beach,1984	12	--	--	--	Tierra Verde, FL
Wally Dallenbach,Jr.	27	N/A	Road America,1987	4	--	--	--	Basalt, CO
Mark Dismore	34	Arciero	--	0	--	--	--	Greenfield, IN
Dominic Dobson	31	N/A	Laguna Seca,1985	36	--	--	--	Fairfax, CA
Teo Fabi	35	N/A	Atlanta,1983	66	9	Pocono,1983	5	Milan, Italy
Emerson Fittipaldi	44	Penske	Long Beach,1984	102	8	Michigan,1985	12	Miami, FL
Stan Fox	38	Hemelgarn	Milwaukee,1984	8	--	--	--	Janesville, WI
A.J. Foyt, Jr.	56	Foyt	Springfield,1957	350	53	Duquoin,1960	67	Houston, TX
Scott Goodyear	31	UNO	Meadowlands,1987	23	--	--	--	Toronto, Canada
Mike Groff	29	N/A	Detroit,1990	12	--	--	--	Studio City, CA
Michael Greenfield	26	N/A	Cleveland,1990	5	--	--	--	Manhasset, NY
Roberto Guerrero	32	N/A	Long Beach,1984	99	5	Phoenix,1987	2	San Juan Capistrano, CA
Dean Hall	33	N/A	Phoenix,1990	15	--	--	--	Olympic Valley, CA
John Jones	25	Euromotorsports	Phoenix,1988	28	--	--	--	Thunder Bay, Ont.,Canada
Buddy Lazier	23	N/A	Portland,1990	6	--	--	--	Vail, CO
Randy Lewis	45	Dale Coyne	Laguna Seca,1983	70	--	--	--	Hillsborough, CA
Arie Luyendyk	37	UNO/Granatelli	Road America,1984	87	--	Indianapolis,1990	1	Paradise Valley, AZ
Hiro Matsushita	27	Paragon	Long Beach,1990	7	--	--	--	San Clemente, CA
Rick Mears	39	Penske	Ontario,1976	163	33	Milwaukee,1978	27	Bakersfield, CA
Rocky Moran	41	N/A	Watkins Glen,1981	24	--	--	--	Coto de Caza, CA
Tero Palmroth	38	N/A	Indianapolis,1988	9	--	--	--	Tampere, Finland
John Paul, Jr.	31	Winkelmann	Elkhart Lake,1982	25	1	Michigan,1983	1	West Palm Beach, FL
Scott Pruett	30	TrueSports	Long Beach,1988	18	--	--	--	Dublin, OH
Bobby Rahal	38	Galles/Kraco	Phoenix,1982	132	14	Cleveland,1982	19	Dublin, OH
Willy T. Ribbs	35	N/A	Long Beach,1990	8	--	--	--	San Jose, CA
Franco Scapini	27	Euromotorsports		--	--	--	--	Monte Carlo, Monaco
Tom Sneva	42	N/A	Trenton,1971	205	14	Michigan,1975	13	Paradise Valley, AZ
Danny Sullivan	41	Patrick	Atlanta,1982	110	19	Cleveland,1984	15	Aspen, CO
Didier Theys	32	N/A	Long Beach,1987	35	--	--	--	Nivelles, Belgium
Paul Tracy	22	Dale Coyne	--	--	--	--	--	Toronto, Canada
Al Unser, Sr.	51	Patrick	Milwaukee,1964	315	27	Pikes Peak,1965	39	Albuquerque, NM
Al Unser,Jr.	28	Galles/Kraco	Riverside,1982	123	2	Portland,1984	15	Albuquerque, NM
Jeff Wood	34	N/A	Las Vegas,1983	22	--	--	--	Witchita, KS

A Lap Around Indy

When you ask most Indy car drivers which is their favorite track the answer is almost always Indianapolis. Three-time Indy champion Rick Mears takes us on a tour of the most famous speedway in the world.

Rick Mears: Basically, you roll out of the pits, down pit lane, as you go down the pit lane, assuming the car's already warmed up you don't really worry about that too much. You start getting up to speed, you stay on the apron through turn one and across the short chute as you're gradually building up speed-- you're looking at the gauges, making sure everything is okay. You start picking up the gears, start picking up the throttle--you go through turn two on the apron, start down the back straight. You continue picking up the throttle and start getting the blower, the boost up, continue though the gears. You start checking the mirrors to make sure that you don't see anything in the back of the car that shouldn't be, check for traffic coming up on you, try to find a clear spot, make sure that the track is open. You get up to speed going down the back straightaway. If nobody's around, then you gradually work your way across toward the outside. Usually, my first time down the back straightaway, I may not go all of the way up to the wall to set up for turn three, just in case there is somebody in my blind spot. Cars on that track can come up on you so fast. You can look in the mirror one time and it will be totally clear. You start looking at the gauges or whatever and you think you're clear and you look back and there's somebody on you immediately. The closing rate is so fast when you're getting up to speed, so you continuously check the mirrors.

Rick Amabile: Do you still get in someone's way by accident ?

Mears: Oh yeah, it happens....and you feel like a real idiot !

Amabile: That's when somebody starts shaking their fist at you !

Mears: Yeah, but by not going clear to the wall, even if you do go out there mistakenly, you don't see the guy, he can keep going. He may not even know that you don't know he's there. So he won't shake his fist at you ! (laughing)

Amabile: That way if it's a rookie you won't look bad!

Mears: Right. You learn little things like that, just safety things. It's just something where you get a routine going. So then by the time you go into turn three, you run down in the corner, you're on the gas and up to speed by then, then if you look back and somebody's there, they 're not closing on you real fast because you're up to speed by that point. So you go through three, you're out in the groove by then--you're on the throttle, you just start feeling the car then. You ease it

through turn four because the tires are cold. You pick up the throttle hard down the front straightaway. You back off early going into one on the first lap, the first time through because the tires are still cold. If you've made a change on the car, you want to feel it out. You see what the car tells you in turn one. If everything's still okay, you pick the throttle up a little bit more in turn two. You run the same pattern, out against the wall going in, down on the apron through the middle, back out to the wall on the exit of two. Then you're on it pretty hard. You progress through turn two, whatever the car tells you then, that gives you an indicator of how hard you can hit turn three. But you usually still aren't up to top speed yet.

Amabile: How long does it take to get the tires all warmed up ?

Mears: It depends on the tire, they change it from year to year. Sometimes they come in right away, sometimes it takes three or four laps. It just depends on the compound and the construction of the tire.

Amabile: Can you feel each mile per hour, or even a half mile per hour at 220 mph ?

Mears: Yeah, I can. You spend all month there refining, you're trying to get every fraction. After you spend that much time on the track, there's indicators in the car that let you know, one being the steering wheel. To me, the steering wheel is the biggest indicator that you have. How much loads on the wheel, how much angle you're turning in--feeling the tire directly to the pavement, that's the biggest indicator you have: that can tell you if the car is loose, neutral, or pushing without ever slipping a tire. Instead of waiting for the car to slip to find out, the steering wheel will tell you if you listen.

Amabile: Does that just go with experience ?

Mears: Yeah, it just takes time.

Amabile: Do you ever notice the crowd, the color and the blur and everything ?

Mears: At times. If you aren't on a flat out lap, you can look around a little bit-- at the right time and the right place. Obviously you don't do it in the middle of the corner or at the entry. The entry is the key. Your entry determines your exit. If you get the entry wrong, your exit's wrong. So that's one of the key times.

Amabile: If you're off on your entry, do you just back off a little ?

Mears: Yeah, you can tell immediately if you're wrong. A lot of drivers will wait until they get to the other end of the corner, and find out they're really wrong before they do something about it. My heart won't take that! If I know that it's a little wrong, I'm going to correct it before I get to the exit, whether that's lifting or turning different then I normally would or whatever the case. I don't like scaring myself any more than I have to !